STARTING WITH HEGEL

Continuum's *Starting with . . .* series offers clear, concise and access-ible introductions to the key thinkers in philosophy. The books explore and illuminate the roots of each philosopher's work and ideas, leading readers to a thorough understanding of the key influences and philosophical foundations from which his or her thought developed. Ideal for first-year students starting out in phil-osophy, the series will serve as the ideal companion to study of this fascinating subject.

Available now:

Starting with Berkeley, Nick Jones

Starting with Derrida, Sean Gaston

Starting with Descartes, C. G. Prado

Starting with Hobbes, George MacDonald Ross

Starting with Nietzsche, Ullrich Haase

Starting with Rousseau, James Delaney

Forthcoming:

Starting with Heidegger, Thomas Greaves

Starting with Hume, Charlotte R. Brown and
    William Edward Morris

Starting with Kant, Andrew Ward

Starting with Kierkegaard, Patrick Sheil

Starting with Leibniz, Roger Woolhouse

Starting with Locke, Greg Forster

Starting with Merleau-Ponty, Katherine Morris

Starting with Mill, John R. Fitzpatrick

Starting with Sartre, Gail Linsenbard

Starting with Wittgenstein, Chon Tejedor

STARTING WITH HEGEL

CRAIG B. MATARRESE

continuum

Continuum International Publishing Group
The Tower Building   80 Maiden Lane
11 York Road   Suite 704
London SE1 7NX   New York, NY 10038

www.continuumbooks.com

British Library Cataloguing-in-Publication Data
A catalogue record for this book is available from the British Library.

ISBN: HB: 978-1-8470-6201-7
PB: 978-1-8470-6202-4

Library of Congress Cataloging-in-Publication Data
Matarrese, Craig B.
Starting with Hegel / Craig B. Matarrese.
p. cm.
Includes bibliographical references (p.   ) and index.
ISBN 978-1-8470-6201-7 – ISBN 978-1-8470-6202-4
1. Hegel, Georg Wilhelm Friedrich, 1770–1831.   I. Title.

B2948.M315 2009
193–dc22

2009015846

Typeset by RefineCatch Limited, Bungay, Suffolk
Printed and bound in Great Britain by
the MPG Books Group

CONTENTS

CHAPTER 4: HEGEL'S *ENCYCLOPEDIA*: THE
STRUCTURE OF BEING, NATURE, AND MIND

CHAPTER 5: THE *PHILOSOPHY OF RIGHT*:
FREEDOM AS SELF-REALIZATION

CHAPTER 6: THE PHILOSOPHY OF HISTORY:
REASON RULES THE WORLD

CHAPTER 7: ABSOLUTE SPIRIT: ART, RELIGION,
AND PHILOSOPHY

ABBREVIATIONS

WORKS BY HEGEL

D   *The Difference Between Fichte's and Schelling's System of Philosophy* (translation of *Differenz des Fichte'schen und Schelling'schen Systems der Philosophie*). Trans. H. S. Harris and Walter Cerf. Albany, NY: SUNY Press, 1977.

ENCI   *The Encyclopaedia Logic.* Trans. Geraets, Suchtung and Harris. Indianapolis, IN: Hackett Publishing Co., Inc., 1991. Cited by section number; Vol. I includes §§ 1–244.

ENCII   *Hegel's Philosophy of Nature.* Trans. A. V. Miller. Oxford: Clarendon Press, 1970. Cited by section number; Vol. II includes §§ 245–376.

ENCIII   *Hegel's Philosophy of Mind.* Trans. A.V. Miller. Oxford: Clarendon Press, 1973. Cited by section number; Vol. III includes §§ 377–577.

HAI, HAII   *Aesthetics: Lectures on Fine Art* by Georg Wilhelm Friedrich Hegel and T. M. Knox. Trans. T. M. Knox. Edition: reprint, illustrated and published by Oxford University Press, 1998.

ETW   *Early Theological Writings.* Trans. T. M. Knox. Philadelphia, PA: University of Pennsylvania, 1975.

FK   *Faith & Knowledge.* Trans. Walter Cerf and H. S. Harris. Albany, NY: State University of New York Press, 1977.

HPW	*Hegel's Political Writings.* Trans. T. M. Knox. Oxford: Clarendon Press, 1964.
ILA	*Introductory Lectures on Aesthetics.* Ed. Michael Inwood. Trans. Bernard Bosanquet. London: Penguin Books, 1993.
JSII	*Werke, Bd. 2: Jenaer Schriften 1801–1907 (Werke in zwanzig Bänden*, ed. Eva Moldenhauer and Karl Markus Michel, Frankfurt a. M.: Suhrkamp, 1979, Vol. 2). Cited by page number; the passage cited is also published in translation as 'Aphorisms from the Wastebook,' in *The Independent Journal of Philosophy*, Vol. 3, 1979.
L	*Love* (in *The Hegel Reader*, ed. Stephen Houlgate. Malden, MA: Blackwell, 1998).
LHP	*Lectures on the History of Philosophy, Vol. I.* Trans. E. S. Haldane. Lincoln, NE: University of Nebraska Press, 1995.
LNR	*Lectures on Natural Right and Political Science: The First Philosophy of Right, Heidelberg 1817–1818 with Additions from the Lectures of 1818–1819.* Transcribed by Peter Wannenmann. Edited by the Staff of the Hegel Archives. Translated by J. Michael Stewart and Peter C. Hodgson. Berkeley, CA: University of California Press, 1995. Cited by section number.
LPH	*Lectures on the Philosophy of World History: Introduction.* Trans. H. B. Nisbet. Introduction by Duncan Forbes. Cambridge: Cambridge University Press, 1975.
LPRI	*Lectures on the Philosophy of Religion.* Trans. R. F. Brown, P. C. Hodgson, J. M. Stewart and H. S. Harris. Berkeley, CA: University of California Press, 1988.
NL	*Natural Law: The Scientific Ways of Treating Natural Law, Its Place in Moral Philosophy, and Its Relation to the Positive Sciences of Law.* Trans. T. M. Knox. Philadelphia, PA: University of Pennsylvania Press, 1975.

ABBREVIATIONS

PH	*The Philosophy of History.* Preface by Charles Hegel. Trans. J. Sibree. New York: Dover Publications, Inc.
PHG	*The Phenomenology of Spirit.* Trans. by A. V. Miller. Oxford: Oxford University Press, 1977. Cited by section number.
PR	*Elements of the Philosophy of Right.* Cambridge: Cambridge University Press, 1991.
SEL	*System of Ethical Life.* Ed. and Trans. H. S. Harris and T. M. Knox. Albany, NY: State University of New York Press, 1979.
SL	*Hegel's Science of Logic.* Trans. A. V. Miller. Ed. H. D. Lewis. Atlantic Highlands, NJ: Humanities Press International, Inc., 1989.

OTHER TEXTS CITED

DE	Aristotle. *De Anima.* Trans. by W. S. Hett. Cambridge, MA: Harvard University Press, 1986.
NE	Aristotle. *Nicomachean Ethics.* Trans. Terence Irwin. Indianapolis, IN: Hackett Publishing Co., 1985.
HF	Berlin, Isaiah. *The Hedgehog and the Fox: An Essay on Tolstoy's View of History.* New York: Simon and Schuster, 1986.
DD	Dennett, Daniel. *Darwin's Dangerous Idea: Evolution and the Meanings of Life.* New York: Simon and Schuster, 1996.
PRG	James, William. *Pragmatism,* Indianapolis, IN: Hackett Publishing Co., 1981.
CJ	Kant, Immanuel. *The Critique of the Power of Judgment.* Cambridge: Cambridge University Press, 2000. Cited by section number.
CPR	Kant, Immanuel. *Critique of Practical Reason.* Cambridge: Cambridge University Press, 1997. Cited by volume and page number from the Berlin Edition.
KPR	Kant, Immanuel. *Critique of Pure Reason, 2nd edition.* Trans. Norman Kemp Smith. Citation to Preface [P] and page numbers.

KS	Kant, Immanuel. *Kant: Selections*. Ed. Lewis White Beck. Upper Saddle River, NJ: Prentice Hall, 1988.
GMM	Kant, Immanuel. *Metaphysics of Morals*. Cambridge Texts in the History of Philosophy. Cambridge: Cambridge University Press, 1996. Volume and page number correlate with *Immanuel Kants Schriften*. Ausgabe der königlich preussischen Akademie der Wissenschaften. Berlin: W. de Gruyter, 1902–.
PFM	Kant, Immanuel. *Prolegomena to Any Future Metaphysics*. Trans. Lewis White Beck. Indianapolis, IN: Bobbs-Merrill, 1950 now MacMillan. Page numbers standard edition of the German text, the *Akademie* edition, Vol. IV, Berlin, 1911.
GS	Nietzsche, Friedrich. *The Gay Science*. Trans. Walter Kaufmann. New York: Vintage Books, 1974. Cited by section number.
OSI	Popper, Karl. *The Open Society and Its Enemies, Vol. I* (originally published in 1945), Princeton, NJ: Princeton University press, 1971.
OSII	Popper, Karl. *The Open Society and its Enemies: Hegel and Marx, 5th edition*. London: Routledge, 2003.
PP	Russell, Bertrand. *The Problems of Philosophy*. Wilder Publications, 2008.
PI	Wittgenstein, Ludwig. *Philosophical Investigations*. Trans. G. E. M. Anscombe. New York: Macmillan, 1958. Cited by section number.

OTHER WORKS MENTIONED

Boccaccio, Giovanni. *The Decameron*. Classics, Revised edition, 2003.

Capellanus, Andreas. *The Art of Courtly Love*. Trans. John Jay Parry. New York: Columbia University Press, 1990.

Coleman, Ornette. *Free Jazz*. Original release date, 21 Dec. 1960. Atlantic Records.

Darwin, Charles. *The Origin of Species*. 150th anniversary edition, Signet Classics, 2003.

Diamond, Jared. *Guns, Germs, and Steel: The Fates of Human Societies*. New York: W. W. Norton & Co., 1997.

Dostoyevsky, Fyodor. *Notes from the Underground*. Critical Studies in Russian Literature. Bristol: Bristol Classical Press, 1993.

Goethe, Johann Wolfgang. *Faust: A Tragedy*. Norton Critical edition. New York: W. W. Norton, 2000.

Goethe, Johann Wolfgang. *Wilhelm Meister's Apprenticeship*. Whitefish, MT: Kessinger Publishing, LLC, 2007.

Lessing, Gotthold. *Nathan the Wise*. Dodo Press, 2009. Originally published in 1779.

Marie de France. *The Lais of Marie de France*. London: Penguin Classics, 2nd edition, 1999.

Marx, Karl. *Capital*. Moscow: Progress Publishers, 1954.

Marx, Karl & Friedrich Engels. *Collected Works*. New York: International Publishers, 1975.

Schiller, Friedrich. *On the Aesthetic Education of Man*. Trans. Reginald Snell. Bristol: Thoemmes Press, 1994.

Sophocles, *Antigone*. Clayton, DE: Prestwick House, Inc., 2005.

CHAPTER 1

INTRODUCTION

Reading the newspaper in early morning is a kind of realistic morning prayer. One orients one's attitude against the world and toward God, or toward that which the world is. The former gives the same security as the latter, in that one knows where one stands. (JSII 547)

Since the beginning of the Western intellectual tradition, philosophy has always been characterized by two fundamental and opposing drives. One leads philosophers to construct sweeping, ambitious, and audacious theories, complete with unitary organizing principles of limitless application, and deep commitments to idealism and optimism; the other motivates philosophers to exercise the doubt and caution appropriate to modern scientific methodology, aspiring most of all to be precise, measured, and attentive to the messy details and heterogeneity of experience. The nineteenth-century American philosopher William James once described these dispositions as 'tender-minded' and 'tough-minded' accordingly (PRG 10); and Sir Isaiah Berlin, the twentieth-century British philosopher, added the colorful designations of the 'hedgehog' and the 'fox,' following the ancient Greek poet Archilochus, who said 'the fox knows many things, but the hedgehog knows one big thing' (HF 3–5). It may be true that most philosophers have intuitions that seem to fit one or the other drive, but in most contexts the opposition will be an obvious oversimplification. In any case, philosophy needs both drives, since each expands our knowledge and understanding of ourselves and the world, and since each tends to check the excesses of the other.

In the history of philosophy, though, there have certainly been stretches of time where one drive seemed to overpower the other, only to be decisively checked by the eventual re-emergence of the opposing disposition. So, for example, the ancient Greek philosophers Anaximander (610–546 BCE), Pythagoras (571–497 BCE), and Heraclitus (~500 BCE) were 'tender-minded' hedgehogs: they took themselves to be developing scientific views of the universe, but at the time, this involved postulating basic principles with expansive scope and application, and the assumption that human reason and human understanding had no limits. But it was not long before Socrates (470–399 BCE) started questioning such claims to knowledge, with remarkable attention to the finer points of meaning and language, and a genuine commitment to intellectual honesty. And Socrates taught us the important lesson that however these opposing philosophical drives are characterized, they both yield forms of knowledge: knowing that one does not know ('Socratic ignorance') is itself a kind of knowledge.

With the Enlightenment and the ascendency of modern science through the seventeenth and eighteenth centuries, the 'tough-minded,' skeptical, and empirically oriented disposition came into its own. The French philosopher René Descartes (1596–1650) took it upon himself to doubt absolutely everything, and his efforts were followed by the Scottish philosopher David Hume (1711–76), who integrated skepticism with the emerging model and method of scientific inquiry. And it was Hume who famously awoke Immanuel Kant (1724–1804) from his 'dogmatic slumbers,' leading him radically to reduce the ambitions of reason (PFM 260).

Enter: Georg Wilhelm Friedrich Hegel (1770–1831), the pivotal figure of nineteenth-century German philosophy, whose grand philosophical ambitions and extraordinary talents would lead to his reputation today as the 'tender-minded' hedgehog par excellence. This view of Hegel today is not wrong, but it is stunningly one-sided: he did want philosophy to be as powerful as Anaximander, Pythagoras, and Heraclitus would have imagined, but he also wanted all of the laudable features of the opposing drive. Hegel wanted it all, the 'tender-minded' and the 'tough-minded,' the hedgehog and the fox; he wanted philosophy to be fearless and creative, but also scientific, rigorous, and responsible to all the empirical facts. And he may have been the first philosopher in history so well-positioned to draw on both of these basic philosophical drives in equal measure.

Today's philosophers are for the most part 'tough-minded,' and this is unsurprising given the extraordinary success of the sciences in the twentieth century, which have offered compelling, if incomplete, explanations of everything from the origins of the universe and the evolutionary development of life, to the exquisite intricacies of embryology and the human brain. Such 'tough-minded' intuitions explain in part why, for most of the twentieth century, students of philosophy (in the English-speaking world, at least) were assaulted with any number of obtrusively unhelpful comments about Hegel's philosophy; for example, Bertrand Russell and Karl Popper both made sloppy, specious, and inexcusable comments about Hegel that poisoned the well for the whole generations of young philosophers (PP 116–19; OSI 121, 144, 161; OSII 32, 41, 64, 245). But Hegel deserves a fair reading, more than just our initial, one-sided reactions that stem from our contemporary intuitions; and we are obligated to give him this fair reading if we are to reach anything like a judicious assessment of his philosophy.

In the process of carrying out this fair assessment, we might consider that Hegel's philosophy is something of a master key to unlocking almost every major trend of the Western intellectual tradition since the middle of the nineteenth century. In the various reactions to Hegelian philosophy, both positive and negative, one finds the intellectual roots of postmodernism, critical theory, Marxism, existentialism, phenomenology, pragmatism, and communitarianism; Jürgen Habermas, Herbert Marcuse, Hans-Georg Gadamer, Jean-Francois Lyotard, Jean-Paul Sartre, Michael Foucault, John Dewey, and even Jaques Derrida, to name a few, are all reacting in specific ways to Hegel's philosophy. Even many contemporary philosophers working in analytic philosophy (e.g., Robert Brandom and John McDowell) and feminism (e.g., Judith Butler, Nancy Fraser, Drucilla Cornell, and less recent but still worth mentioning, Simone de Beauvoir) draw on Hegel in one way or another. Anyone with an interest in these recent intellectual trends will want a good understanding of what Hegel was up to.

We might also notice that Hegelian philosophy has a direct bearing on a wide range of today's questions and issues that emerge in philosophy as well as other disciplines. Professional philosophers are certainly aware of this, as evidenced by the explosion of interest in and writings on Hegel starting in the 1970s, and have brought Hegel into discussions of social and political philosophy, epistemology, and the philosophy of mind and language. Aside from philosophers, Hegel's writings are read today by theoretical physicists, evolutionary biologists, child psychologists, public policy experts, environmentalists, lawyers, and musicians, among others. Hegel recognized no rigid disciplinary boundary between philosophy, political science, history, economics, or any other discipline, so it is perhaps not surprising that his work has emerged and proven useful in all of these areas.

But we should not forget that aside from any academic concerns, Hegel thought that philosophy could make a difference in the lives of ordinary people. He thought that any human being is, at least implicitly, committed to some philosophical interpretation or other of the world, and that this invites a number of questions. On that interpretation, what is the goal or end of human life? How are we trying to attain it? And how will we know when we get there? Is it anyway a justifiable goal to have? Hegel thinks that we are most likely to miss those features of our thinking and of the world that are most familiar to us, because they are 'right under our noses'; philosophy must take 'common sense' seriously, as a philosophically rich interpretation of the world that both reveals and conceals the structure of our thought. We should want to understand this structure, Hegel urges, because it often contains contradictions and tensions that ultimately cause human suffering. And philosophy is the discipline that is most skilled at analyzing these structures, and diagnosing the problems that may emerge.

Hegelian philosophy is a living philosophy today not just because it was self-consciously built on the best insights of the previous two millennia of philosophical inquiry, but because its interpretive and historical method pushes us to develop the most comprehensive and satisfying explanation of what we moderns are up to, how we came to think the way we do, and how we came to have the values and interests we currently take so seriously. Of course, this really is a philosopher's ambition, to embrace the Herculean (i.e., Hegelian) task of constructing an interpretation so comprehensive that we question whether we can bear the rigors of our own theory. We may, in the end, be unable to satisfy the ambitions of Hegelian philosophy; but any efforts towards that end, regardless of our estimation of their success, repay us richly. But we cannot think that our story will look like Hegel's: much has happened in the last one-hundred and eighty years, and our ways of interpreting ourselves have become deeper and more sophisticated. Doing Hegelian philosophy today means reinterpreting the same events and ideas that Hegel considered, along with what has happened since then, and all from our currently situated point of view.

Any attempt to substantiate all of these claims about Hegel's importance and contemporary relevance must be based on the serious consideration of each of Hegel's major works; this chapter is an introduction to this project, and includes first (i) a brief recounting of Hegel's life, works, and predecessors, followed by an account of the two most important thematic concerns that run through all of Hegel's philosophy: (ii) his speculative hermeneutics, and (iii) his notion of organic unity and development. At the end of this chapter, I will also (iv) give some indication of the overall structure of this book, and the ideas that will be covered in each chapter.

i. THE FALLING OF DUSK

Hegel argues that philosophy is essentially a backward-looking and reconstructive type of interpretation, which pays special attention to the way our values, questions and interests have come to have their current meaning for us. Understanding how our ideas have originated in and developed through history, he asserts, is a necessary condition for really knowing who we are and what we are up to. Hegel's philosophy is deeply historicist, and although he defends this basic orientation without reference to his personal experiences, it would nonetheless seem reasonable to suspect that the dramatic and portentous events that shaped his generation's hopes, ambitions, and fears, had some impact on his philosophical dispositions. In any case, we can reconstruct the philosophical questions and problems that shaped Hegel's career, as an interpretive exercise consistent with the principles of his own view, and try to discern whether they were adopted straightaway from his predecessors, or whether they had been modified in crucial ways as they were taken up.

Hegel was born in 1770 in Stuttgart, Germany, and witnessed at the brink of adulthood the French Revolution, the uncertain apex of Enlightenment rationalism, the prodigious industrialization and growth of market economies, and the quickly shifting ground of European culture and politics. The Enlightenment ideals of universal rationality and secular humanism that animated the French Revolution, along with Napoleon's increasing power and imperial expansion, provoked an especially strong counter-reaction in Germany, which took the form of romanticism: the celebration of individuality, art, mysticism, and traditional culture seemed to be the only viable form of resistance. Even though Germany was comprised of scattered principalities, most of which were corrupt and oppressive, part of the romantic counter-Enlightenment took the form of nationalism; but since no unified Germany had yet emerged since the disintegration of the Holy Roman Empire, this romantic proto-nationalism could only be based on a hopeful yet indeterminate possibility. In any case, as strong as romanticism was in Germany, there was at least as much support for the changes that seemed imminent. Hegel's early education was saturated by the principles of the Enlightenment, but he certainly felt the pull of romanticism as well; some degree of ambivalence would anyway be appropriate for one growing up in Germany at the intersection of these political and cultural cross currents.

The period stretching from the French Revolution in 1789 to about 1830 was a philosophical revolution as well, with German philosophers seeming to steal the show from France, thus taking the lead in the cultural and intellectual changes then sweeping across Europe. The dominant philosophical figure in Germany was Kant, who radicalized the entire project of metaphysics and epistemology by arguing against the commonsensical notion that the external world is both independent from us and knowable through reason. In *The Critique of Pure Reason* (1781), Kant argues that all of the basic features of human experience are actually our own contributions, not features of the world apart from us; even space and time are fabrications of our own minds, the necessary conditions for the possibility of any experience whatever. Kant describes his revolutionary move as 'Copernican' because he turned the tables in much the same way as Copernicus did in defending the heliocentric over the geocentric view of the universe: everything changes once we acknowledge that the observer contributes to the observation (KPRB xvi). After Kant, the knowing subject could no longer be considered the passive recipient of information about the world; rather, the subject is now seen as actively imposing structure on experience. And since reason cannot escape the structure of our own imposed categories of experience and judgement, we can only ever have knowledge of things as they appear to us, as 'phenomena,' and whatever it is that exists beyond them, the 'noumenal' world, is completely unknowable to us.

For Kant, then, we cannot know anything about the external world through reason, so the very ambitions of reason must be reined in and strictly limited. But attenuating the domain of reason in this way, Kant says, actually makes room for other sorts of claims, which might be applied to morality and religion. He thought that there were a number of things we could say, or postulate on behalf of the moral point of view, that were not claims of reason, but were nonetheless still interesting and important. Specifically, he thought that if morality was to make any sense at all, we had to postulate that we each had a free will, that the soul was immortal, and that God exists. These claims are not provable by reason, but we must accept them anyway, as conditions for the possibility of morality. Kant specifies these postulates in his 'second critique,' *The Critique of Practical Reason* (1787), which restates some of the arguments about morality that appear in his earlier book, *Groundwork for the Metaphysics of Morals* (CPR 5: 122). It is in these books that Kant defends the 'categorical imperative,' a moral principle that is intended to be universally valid for all of humanity: act only where one can will the maxim of that act to be universal moral law. This is just one of many formulations of the 'categorical imperative' that Kant considers, though, a more intuitive formulation is: always treat people as ends-in-themselves, and never as means only (GMM 4: 402–03, 428–30).

Perhaps more important than the particularities of the 'categorical imperative', though, is Kant's new conception of what it means to be a human being. On his view, the two most important features of being human are that we each have a free will, and that we are rational. It is because we are both free and rational that we can understand what moral duty requires of us, and act in genuinely moral ways; it is for the same reason that we have a special moral standing in the world, an absolute value as human beings that ought not be violated or undermined. But since Kant accepted a mechanistic conception of nature bound by Newtonian laws, he could only defend our having a free will by claiming for it a distinct metaphysical status. Our will, Kant argues, exists simultaneously in two worlds: spontaneously and independently, outside of the laws of physics, as the will (*Wille*) of our 'noumenal' self, and also as the will (*Willkür*) of the empirically determined world, as part of our 'phenomenal' self (KPP A577–78).

Kant was not the first philosopher to argue that freedom and rationality were the essential features of human selfhood; the full story of the Enlightenment conception of selfhood would, at least, have to begin with Descartes, and follow the contributions and questions of Hume and Jean-Jacques Rousseau (1712–78), to show the origins and growing instability of this conception of selfhood. Starting with Descartes, the self acquired a new transcendental and universal status, and became responsible for constituting or at least mediating our whole experience of the world and of other selves in it. This conception of selfhood was both narrow, because it focused on the will and reason to the exclusion of all else that might be relevant, and extraordinarily optimistic, because it assumed that our freedom was absolute and that our rationality was the executive faculty of mind, unfettered by the passions, supremely empowered, and transparent in operation. By the time of Kant's mature writings, though, this conception of selfhood was already crumbling under the weight of Hume's skeptical challenge to the supremacy of reason, and also in light of Rousseau's romantic politicization of the self. Kant's project, then, should be considered as something of a last ditch effort to save this Enlightenment self that started with Descartes: it was only with a drastically limited domain that reason could make good on its claims, and only with an elaborate set of 'postulations' that we could save morality and religion as we knew them.

It should not be surprising, then, that Kant had a much greater impact on the next generation (Hegel's generation) than his own, since his view was both radical and something of a death knell, yielding indigestible fare for his contemporaries. It took a younger generation to see that the Enlightenment conception of the self had reached its terminus in Kant: the inflated ambition that the 'self' was transcendental, universal, transparent, and unbound by the laws of nature, had exhausted itself. Hegel would later have a special interest in the openings that these historical transitions allow; as he would put in the *Philosophy of Right*, 'the owl of Minerva begins its flight only with the onset of dusk' (PR 23). In the context of intellectual, cultural, and historical change, this means that real moments of clarity are possible only when an age is moribund, when its aims and questions have played themselves out, and the next age waits to sever its ties with a qualitative break.

Hegel's first step into this fray took him to the seminary in Tübingen, where he studied from 1788 to 1793, and seemed to be on his way to becoming a Protestant minister. This was a well-worn career path in Hegel's family, but during his seminary years, Hegel came to reject the dogmatism of traditional theology as well as the widespread institutionalized corruption that supported it. He had already been influenced by the writings of Gotthold Lessing (1729–81) prior to attending the seminary, and had been modelling his career aspirations after Lessing's role as a public intellectual. Lessing had certainly influenced a broad audience through books like *Nathan the Wise* (published in 1779), which suggested ways that traditional religion might be reconciled with the ideals of Enlightenment rationality. Hegel imagined a similar role for himself, and though the ministry would be a plausible backdrop for this, his intuitions had long pulled him towards philosophy; and this trajectory was strengthened by two new friendships, with Friedrich Hölderlin (1770–1843), who would later become an important romantic poet, and Friedrich Wilhelm Joseph von Schelling (1775–1854), who would quickly rise to prominence as a philosopher of nature (Schelling had great success very early in his career, and this would generate tension with Hegel, whose career had a much slower start). All three were enthusiastic supporters of the French Revolution and Napoleon, and energized by the apparent dawning of a new era.

Hegel's most interesting piece of writing from this period, an unpublished fragment now commonly referred to as the 'Tübingen essay,' addresses the role of religion in public life. Stemming from his rejection of theological dogmatism, Hegel argues that if religion were to have a positive effect on people and help them to overcome the fragmentation of modern life, it would have to become a genuine 'people's religion' (*Volksreligion*) that moved beyond dogmatism and superstition, and somehow brought people's personal sentiments into a functional harmony with their cultural and political institutions. Despite his enthusiasm for the Enlightenment valorization of reason, Hegel did not think that cultural fragmentation could be overcome by reason alone; something had to reach people's hearts in addition to their minds, and the best way to do this, he thought, was through an enlightened and politically engaged 'people's religion'.

In 1793, Hegel completed his seminary studies and moved to Berne, where he took up a job as a private tutor. Although Hegel felt isolated in Berne, and missed the company of his friends, Schelling and Hölderlin, he was nonetheless very productive with his writing. During this period, Hegel wrote *The Positivity of the Christian Religion* (typically referred to as the '*Positivity* essay'), *The Life of Jesus*, and *The Earliest System-Programme of German Idealism*. Hegel's treatment of Christianity in these writings is uniformly critical, and his arguments are strongly influenced by his reading of Kant (who was also critical of institutionalized Christianity): Hegel argued that Jesus was actually a kind of proto-Kantian, who tried to defend reason and a rationalistic conception of the moral law, but whose message was lost in the institutional pressures and exigencies of early Christianity. With these pressures at work, Hegel says, Jesus' message became a mere appeal to authority, which is why the more appropriate teacher of humanity and leader of a people's religion would be the Greek philosopher Socrates.

Although Hegel's interpretation of Christianity at this point seems to rest on an unqualified acceptance of Kant's ethics, he and his contemporaries were actually wrestling with a number of problems and tensions in Kant's philosophy, and their ambivalence about it was deepening. They tended to agree with the basic transcendental argument that experience presupposes certain categories of thought, but wondered whether Kant had correctly grasped what these categories were. They were also concerned with what seemed like an entirely awkward and asystematic split between the 'phenomenal' and the 'noumenal' world; they found it bothersome that Kant needed to posit and refer to an entirely unknowable world. But rather than reject the Kantian view wholesale, most young philosophers in the 1790s wanted to fix or 'complete' Kant's system.

One notable attempt to 'complete' Kant's system was already being carried out by Johann Gottlieb Fichte (1762–1814), who had also studied in Tübingen while Hegel was there, but had moved to Jena in 1794 to take a position as a philosophy professor. Fichte greatly admired Kant, and began his career by defending and applying Kant's ethics to religion. His move to Jena, though, was actually a lucky case of brilliance by association: an essay of his went to press without his name on it, and after most readers initially assumed that it was written by Kant himself, Fichte's career promptly took off. Hegel and Schelling both thought of Fichte as the legitimate heir to Kant, and as the only one who would successfully resolve the contradictions in the Kantian system. Fichte's main contribution was to reinterpret the subject as more fundamentally active than Kant had imagined: it is not just that the knowing subject constitutes the structure of its own experience, but moreover that the subject only does this while actually acting in and against the world. Fichte argued that the subject must project its intentions into the material world through action. This active, struggling, and striving self comes to have a very different relationship to the externally existing world than Kant had envisioned, and comes to know the material world as it pushes back against its actions. Fichte also claimed that there was a reality beyond sensation, a 'supersensible' reality that was inward and personal, and could be accessed by way of moral conscience; this was important because it was an innovative way to deny that substance or materiality was the primary stuff of reality, a move that will be taken up by Schelling, Hegel, and others.

As more young philosophers came to see Kant's system as lopsidedly rationalistic, and as romanticism in Germany increased in strength, another philosopher whose project was already well underway moved to center stage. Friedrich Schiller (1759–1805), a philosopher, poet, writer, and well-known defender of secular humanism, argued that the main problem with Kant's view was his bifurcated conception of selfhood: the Kantian self had two utterly separate and opposed sides, a split between the rational and the natural, or phrased differently, between the soul and the body. For Schiller, this was a kind of anti-humanism because it only acknowledged and celebrated one aspect of humanity to the exclusion of any and all other aspects. In a series of short essays written in the 1790s, titled *On the Aesthetic Education of Man*, Schiller argued that our humanity, comprehensively understood to include passions, intuitions, and creativity, in addition to reason, finds its highest expression in art. Schiller was a close friend of Johann Wolfgang von Goethe (1749–1832), author of *Faust* and hugely influential figure in German literature and arts, and argued that Goethe offered a better ideal for humanity than Kant, because Goethe represented the perfect unification of reason and art.

Schiller was arguing that Kantian rationality was one-sided, and that our approach should rather be 'anthropological,' in the sense that it will treat us as complex wholes that are part nature, with animal drives and such, and part reason. Hegel and others thought that Schiller was right about this, and agreed with his efforts to broaden philosophical concerns beyond just the rational, intellectual, and mental. Schiller defended an 'aesthetic' education, which would cultivate the whole person, feelings and passions included, and this would mark his contribution to the general turn away from the traditional concerns of philosophy (metaphysics, knowledge), towards a concern with human practices, institutions, social conditions, history, politics, psychology, and anthropology.

Hegel moved to Frankfurt in 1797, to escape his isolation in Berne and to rejoin Hölderlin, who had been living in Frankfurt, and who arranged for him another job as a private tutor. Hegel was productive during his years in Frankfurt, writing *The Spirit of Christianity and its Fate, Love, The German Constitution*, and *Fragment of a System*, and seemed to be strongly influenced by Hölderlin's romanticism. It was most likely his discussions with Hölderlin that led to his writings on love, his new and more sympathetic approach to religion, and his brief dabbling with mysticism. During this time, Hegel also seems to have adopted Hölderlin's criticism of Fichte, namely that his view went too far in the direction of subjectivism, as well as his view that the only way to resolve the opposition between subject and object was to start with the assumption of a community of knowers. This last point would become crucial for Hegel in the coming years as he starts to work out a view of what we might call 'social epistemology,' or 'social reason'; this was the beginning of Hegel's thinking about 'objective spirit' (*objektiver Geist*), the 'minded' or 'spirited' aspect of social groups that is not reducible to any individual's thoughts or intentions, that he will continue to develop in the years to come.

In 1801, Hegel moved to Jena, now rejoining Schelling, who was teaching at the University of Jena. Hegel started teaching at the University as well, though not in a salaried position, and joined Schelling as co-editor of the *Critical Journal of Philosophy*. Now especially productive, and steering his career trajectory towards becoming a university professor, Hegel wrote *Faith and Knowledge, Natural Law, The Difference between Fichte's and Schelling's Systems of Philosophy* (now typically referred to as the *Differenzschrift*, or the '*Difference* essay'), and the *Phenomenology of Spirit* (often referred to as just the '*Phenomenology*'). Schelling left Jena just two years after Hegel arrived, but it was sufficient time to develop a productive working relationship, one with criticism and contribution running in both directions. Hegel's *Difference* essay, his first publication, was a defense of Schelling's philosophy against Fichte (and Kant); the opposition between realism and idealism, Hegel argues, cannot be overcome unless the opposition itself is rejected in some way, and Fichte and Kant fail to do this. Schelling's answer was to avoid this opposition by starting over with a philosophy of nature, a conception of the organic whole, which then subsumes subject and object, real and ideal, freedom and nature. Hegel agrees with Schelling that whatever unity is to be found in our comprehension of the world must be found through reason (as opposed to intuition or revelation), but he was already developing his own systematic philosophy, forged out of his increasingly critical view of Schelling's ideas about nature.

While in Jena, Hegel struggled to clarify his 'system,' and after a number of false starts and drafts he finally completed what would become his first major work, the *Phenomenology of Spirit*. In that book, he builds on but also separates himself from his predecessors. According to a somewhat apocryphal account, Hegel was finishing the final manuscript and hurriedly leaving Jena just as Napoleon's troops were entering the city in 1806; he may not have actually had Napoleon at his heels, but his situation was certainly dramatic: he had no job, no money, and no plan, and he was within a few months to become a father to an 'illegitimate' son (the mother was Hegel's housekeeper and landlady). In any case, he did relocate to Bamberg for a short time, working as a newspaper editor, before moving to Nuremberg in 1808 to take a job as headmaster of a secondary school, which he hoped would be a stepping-stone to getting a university professor job. While in Nuremberg, Hegel wrote the *Science of Logic* and married Marie von Tucher (with whom he would later have two additional sons).

In 1816, Hegel finally landed a professor job at the University of Heidelberg. He lectured on political philosophy and aesthetics, and wrote the *Encyclopedia of the Philosophical Sciences*, which was the first full version of his 'system.' At this point in his career, Hegel was concerned to make his 'system' as rigorous and scientific as possible, by reworking many of the ideas he adopted from romanticism. Hegel accepted a position at the University of Berlin in 1818, and was enthusiastic about moving there because it seemed to be the center of the ongoing Prussian Reform Movement, which was built around a set of liberal political initiatives. But less than a year after Hegel's arrival in Berlin, Friedrich Wilhelm III clamped down on reform, initiated censorship, and many of Hegel's students were ejected from the University or thrown into prison. Despite these political tensions, and his uneasy relationship with the Prussian establishment, Hegel published the *Philosophy of Right*, and enjoyed increasing popularity through his public lectures on history, religion, and aesthetics. He also worked on new editions of the *Encyclopedia* and the *Logic*. But in 1831, he suddenly became ill and died; there was a cholera epidemic underway at the time, but it is not clear whether Hegel's illness was connected to it.

ii. SPECULATIVE HERMENEUTICS

One central and thematic idea that runs through all of Hegel's philosophy might be called his 'speculative hermeneutics,' which is in part a method of doing philosophy, and in part the expression of a number of substantive value judgments and commitments. A 'hermeneutics' is a theory of interpretation, and a 'speculative' hermeneutics is one that seeks to reconstruct the essential structure of the thing being interpreted (ENCI §§ 79–82). The essential structure that is revealed is what Hegel calls 'reason' or 'rationality,' and it is to be distinguished from all that is contingent, accidental, or merely possible; the 'rational' is what exists with necessity and really matters in the world, and so deserves to be called 'actual' (ENCI § 6; PR 20). Speculative hermeneutics, then, attempts to reveal 'the rational in the real,' which is a shorthand reference to Hegel's assertion that 'what is rational is actual; and what is actual is rational'; and he wants this to be construed as broadly as possible: 'to comprehend *what is* is the task of philosophy, for *what is* is reason (PR 20–21). When we approach an object of interpretation, our task, according to speculative hermeneutics, is to portray that object as maximally rational and coherent; any interpretive approach that refuses to do this, Hegel says, is either arrogant, or profoundly confused about the ways that we are all deeply entrenched in history (PR 21–22).

There are a number of different ideas and arguments packed into the notion of speculative hermeneutics, along with some complexities generated by Hegel's terminology, so let us consider how it might be analyzed into separate claims. Speculative hermeneutics is: descriptive, normative, and critical; bound by the historical mediation of our ideas and criticisms; and productive of an attitude of reconciliation towards our world.

First, speculative hermeneutics based on the notion that the 'rational is actual' is both descriptive and critical. As Hegel might put it, it does not do away with the distinction between 'what a thing has in it to become' and 'what a thing currently happens to be.' Whether Hegel is considering the state, history, nature, or a particular mode of consciousness, he typically focuses on the 'rationality' of the thing in question, by which he means the structure or basic organizing principles of that thing. For example, consider the game of chess. What is the 'rationality' of chess? The basic normative structure of chess is captured by its rules, and these rules make chess what it is. That is to say, it does not really matter what the pieces and the board are made of, whether wood, marble, or something else, nor does it matter who in particular is playing the game. If we observed two people playing chess badly, and with some confusion about the rules, we would not become anxious about whether or not 'chess' exists anymore; and we would not think that the 'rationality' of chess has somehow changed just because these two people are playing poorly or botching the rules. When one uses a speculative hermeneutics to look at chess, the descriptive part of the interpretation involves reconstructing the rules. This might be easy if one is a professional chess master or has access to an official rulebook, but it might otherwise be challenging.

The normative aspect of speculative hermeneutics becomes clear when the basic structure of a thing turns out to be a normative structure of rules, as in the game of chess. But there is a more general way of seeing the normative dimension at work here: speculative hermeneutics presupposes an ideal of coherence, and tries to locate the goal, end, or *telos* in light of this ideal. This just means that when we portray an object as inherently 'rational,' we try to find the goal, or point, that would best explain all the other features of that object; if we think that an object or practice is disjointed, fragmentary, and lacking a discernable point, we have probably failed to portray it as inherently 'rational.' In the chess case, a speculative hermeneutics would try to find some teleological, goal-oriented, scheme that makes sense of the board, the pieces, what the players are doing, and so on. If we are, say, having difficulty capturing the 'rationality' of chess, we may need to take up the internal point of view of its participants in an effort to discern the practice's *telos*. Refusing to depart from the external observer's point of view would make it much easier to develop a destructive, deflationary, and unflattering interpretation, which, in the case of chess, might be that the players are moving pieces randomly, or are doing nothing more than killing time. And, it should be added, the ideal of coherence here is more demanding than those of mere consistency or intelligibility: an object or practice can make sense to us, and be free of blunt contradiction, and yet still lack a point. That is, an interpretation of chess that claimed it to be merely a way of killing time might be an intelligible and non-contradictory one, but a more coherent interpretation would be one that attributed to chess a teleology, and so could better explain how the various features of the practice are systematically interconnected.

It is worth emphasizing the role of the internal perspective in speculative hermeneutics, because it is necessary to carry out 'internal' criticism. It is always easy to criticize a practice or viewpoint from an 'external' point of view, but one must genuinely understand a practice or viewpoint internally if one wants to find weaknesses, tensions, or problems that arise from within that view itself, in light of the goals or aims of that view. The typical internal argument tries to show that a particular view or practice cannot accomplish what it is after, that it cannot succeed on its own terms. This will be an essential mode of argumentation for Hegel, and one that guides his thinking in every domain (PHG §§ 76–79, 80, 84, 87).

If the descriptive work of speculative hermeneutics has already been carried out, and one has a grip on the 'rationality' of the thing under consideration, then one might look to examples of the thing in the world and ask, 'does this thing fully express its rationality, or does it fall short somehow?' This introduces the critical side of speculative hermeneutics, because it allows one to argue that an actually existing thing is failing to express its 'rationality.' So, for example, if one observed two people playing chess badly and violating the rules, one could say that the game exists in degenerate form; the criticism here, that the game has degenerated in this case, is based on the prior assessment of the game's 'rationality,' and the observation that its 'rationality' is not being fully expressed. And we can broaden this case to include the whole culture and institution of chess-playing, where we imagine that chess tournaments are characterized by widespread cheating and where few games are ever finished because players routinely assault each other mid-game. In this broadened case, we would add to the 'rationality' of the game narrowly conceived the 'rationality' of the institutions that are formed around the game, and that have supported it over time. Hegel could interpret this situation with the aim of 'portraying chess as inherently rational,' and thereby consider the norms and practices of chess as they would be at their best, where chess is what it has in it to become; and this would involve both descriptive and critical interpretation.

When Hegel utilizes his speculative hermeneutics in the context of political philosophy, his readers (then and now) will all too often miss the critical dimension of his interpretation. His main work in this area, the *Philosophy of Right*, seems at the first reading to be an entirely descriptive account, and if the reader is not careful to remember that what is being described is the 'rational in the real,' and not just the 'real' by itself, the book appears to be straightforward apologetics. The descriptive part of that book tries to capture how far we moderns have come in our understanding of freedom, and the critical part becomes clear when we see how we are actually falling short of expressing our best understanding of freedom in the actually existing (i.e., 'real') political world. The internal critique of the modern state simply adopts its own criteria, and then shows that the state cannot satisfy them.

Hegel's philosophy is firmly rooted in historicism, and this is the second constitutive claim of speculative hermeneutics; as he puts it: 'each individual is in any case a *child of his time*; thus philosophy, too, is *its own time comprehended in thoughts*' (PR 22). Every idea and interpretation we might come to have, Hegel says, has a history. This does not mean that nothing new ever happens, or that no one is the genuine author of anything; it just means that there is always an historical story to be told, and that this story will contribute to our understanding of whatever it leads up to. This is not a meaningless platitude, because minimally it suggests that we adopt some humility about our current attitudes and values, and implies that this humility is a precondition for a true understanding of who we are. And even philosophy, Hegel claims, cannot step outside of its own time. This will rule out many forms of radical political theory, theories that make sense only if we suppose that people can indeed step outside of their age. For example, utopian theories seem to be speaking to us from the future, just like many romantic theories seem to speak to us from the past; but these theorists cannot avoid speaking from their time, just like we cannot avoid interpreting their theories from our time. Hegel thinks that a serious appreciation of history will rule out many kinds of external criticism: criticizing the status quo from an entirely external vantage point, from some otherworldly or invented point of view, is simply too easy, and will surely end up ignoring whatever dimension of coherence and rationality is already present in the world.

The practical manifestation of this, he thought, is that political change always begins with people as they are, and if change is so dramatic that people cannot render intelligible and embrace the new context they suddenly find themselves in, then instability and backlash are the likely outcomes. The background to this sort of fear for Hegel was his attempt to make sense of the Terror that followed the French Revolution. In the end, Hegel was not a revolutionary, and he defended this position on philosophical grounds. It would be fair to describe Hegel as a moderate liberal reformist: he wanted to promote change, but nothing so radical that people would be suddenly or forcibly torn from the institutional and cultural structures that give their lives meaning and help them force a sense of selfhood.

The third claim entailed by Hegel's speculative hermeneutics is that it produces an attitude of reconciliation with the world. The best indication of this comes from a striking metaphor he uses to describe the philosopher's attitude towards the status quo: 'to recognize reason as the rose in the cross of the present and thereby to delight in the present – this rational insight is the *reconciliation* with actuality which philosophy grants to those who have received the inner call *to comprehend*' (PR 22). Hegel is fully aware of the vast human suffering in the modern world, and thinks that it is an unambiguously bad thing: throughout the *Philosophy of Right*, he points out the many ways that suffering is systemically produced in the modern state, by way of poverty, war, economic instability, alienation, and so on. These are serious problems of course, but instead of gravitating towards resignation, cynicism, and defeat, Hegel instead urges us to find 'the rose' in this mass of suffering, so that in addition to our sadness and melancholy, we may also 'delight in the present.'

But this is not an easy attitude for one to embrace, since it requires that one accept and affirm the world one lives in, while at the same time taking responsibility, as it were, for the corruption, exploitation, hypocrisy, brutality, oppression, and inhumanity, that are all around us. This seems to anticipate what Friedrich Nietzsche (1844–1900) would call, decades later, the attitude of 'life affirmation' or 'love of fate' (GS § 276). Nietzsche, of course, would not be looking to affirm 'reason' in the world, but the sense in which this basically affirmative disposition is a deep sign of strength is something that Hegel and Nietzsche agree on. It takes a certain strength of character to look at what exists, understand that it is corrupt, flawed, incomplete, and so on, but still see within it the structure that expresses what the world has in it to become. This shows something about Hegel's engagement with and optimism about this world, and it will count as one of the most basic themes of his philosophy: that we struggle with a difficult and paradoxical aspiration, a rationalistic *amor fati* coupled with a critical and reconstructive pursuit of coherence.

Hegel's speculative hermeneutics infuses his thinking at all levels, and guides his arguments in every context. He uses this method of interpretation for modes of consciousness in the *Phenomenology of Spirit*, and forms of thought in the *Logic* and *Encyclopedia*. When he considers forms of art and religion through history, he tries to portray them as maximally rational and coherent, and when he examines the modern state in the *Philosophy of Right*, he employs the same method.

iii. ORGANIC UNITY AND SELF-DEVELOPMENT

Hegel uses organic metaphors throughout all of his writings, and constantly returns to the concepts of 'life' and the 'organism' to guide his thinking. 'Organicism' as a philosophical view is usually taken to imply a certain way of thinking about part-whole relations, analogous to the way that organs, limbs, and internal structures are systemically related in a living thing; it might also be described as a kind of anti-reductionism, a resistance to the tendency to break things down into their smallest constituent parts. The idea of 'homeostasis,' the functional stability of a complex biological system, is helpful here because it suggests a dynamic, systemic, and ongoing resolution to internally generated contradictions. For example, the immune system protects the life of the organism, but this sometimes requires that it attack 'itself,' its own tissues, for the sake of the whole; if the contrary force of the immune system goes too far, as in the case of auto-immune diseases, the overarching unity is lost and the organism dies.

The analytic tendency to break 'wholes' into 'parts' is useful, Hegel argues, but we must take responsibility for such interpretations. If we make distinctions between 'reason' and 'emotion,' or 'mind' and 'body,' we cannot then forget that we are dealing with our own creations, abstractions from the whole. In his *Encyclopedia*, Hegel refers to an organic body, in a way that rehearses some of the arguments from Aristotle's *De Anima*: he argues that while a whole is clearly composed of parts, the determination of a part is tantamount to an abandonment of the true meaning of a whole, and amounts to a false and reifying abstraction (for Aristotle, the argument is that an 'ensouled' body is not the sum of its parts). In the *Philosophy of Right*, Hegel refers us to the same reification in his discussion of the nature of human needs: since all human need exists in a social context, one which includes the general coordination of many individuals into a functioning whole, the move to discussing human needs from the isolated and atomized perspective of a single individual (a part from the whole) is a move into the 'untrue' (PR §§ 190–194).

As a methodological issue in the context of political theory, Hegel endorses holism as a starting point: we have a choice to start either with a notion of the individual and work towards the whole, or alternatively, to start with the whole and work towards the individual; here again, Hegel sides with Aristotle (PR § 156). That is, Hegel, like Aristotle, begins with an idea or concept that functions as a starting point (an *archai*) or an origin, which as Aristotle says, is not shown to be the case or defended against rival accounts from the start, but rather shown to be plausible through its exposition (NE 1094a1–1103a11, DA 402b25, 413a16; PR § 2). It is true that such a starting point sounds like a conclusion that seems suspicious because there has been no argumentation for it, but the aspiration is that if one is to develop a systematic approach to a set of problems, the truth of any part would emerge with whatever truth is to be found in the whole through its exposition; Hegel says as much of his philosophy in the Preface to the *Phenomenology* (PHG §§ 24–25, 36–40). The Aristotelian-Hegelian point is that, at least in the realm of political theory, there will always be a comprehensive vision expressed by theory that includes a conception of the self, freedom, the relation of the individual to society, etc., and that this comprehensive vision can be either more or less determinate. The best strategy, then, is not to take one piece of that vision and show that it is true, but rather to articulate the whole vision in the best way possible so that the 'truth' of each part is shown with the 'truth' of the whole.

Another important feature of the organic metaphor is that it is dynamic, and this dynamism is generated in a self-sufficient manner, based on the internal principles of the organism itself. And this is the best way to begin considering what Hegel's 'dialectics' might mean: instead of trying to isolate 'the dialectic' as a formal method, or some 'thing' that apparently has a life of its own, it is much closer to his meaning to see the dialectic as that which unfolds from the internal principles of a thing. When we correctly interpret what an organism, mode of consciousness, or period of history is up to, then we will be able to follow its own developmental path. The key ideas here are: self-organization, self-development, and internal teleology. The dialectic is the structure of the thing or practice playing itself out, of its own inertia; Hegel just tries to make this structure clear and perspicuous.

Hegel uses a biologically-framed metaphor of growth, which he calls *Bildung*, to capture the internal principles and forces that drive development, especially in the case of a human being (though it also applies to humanity considered as a whole). The German word *Bildung* means 'education,' 'cultivation,' or even just 'culture,' and implies that there is some sort of developmental process involved that makes intelligible the move from an uncultivated (or uneducated, uncultured) state to a cultivated one. In this case, it may be better to use the German term, because it contains such a variety of meanings, and because it remains distinct from the related term *Erziehung*, which typically refers to education in the sense of formal schooling; *Bildung* refers to the sort of education one gets through various experiences and encounters in life, which typically, though not always, occur outside of school. There is also the difference that *Bildung* suggests that one must actively place demands on oneself, that one must take on the difficult task of self-formation and self-development, whereas one's *Erziehung* is often taken to be the passive reception of knowledge, something that is received instead of demanded or taken. The implication that one must be actively involved in one's *Bildung* also suggests that 'acculturation' is a potentially misleading translation, since it carries the implication that *Bildung* is something that occurs largely when one is young and being merely impressed upon by society; Hegel's sense of *Bildung* is that, though it must be based on some sort of acculturation, it cannot be limited to this and must include the ability to be critical of one's acculturation. The associated literary genre of the *Bildungsroman*, best exemplified by Goethe's *Faust* or *Wilhelm Meisters Lehrjahre*, captures the broad meaning that Hegel is interested in.

Of course, at the time that Hegel was starting to utilize the idea of *Bildung*, there was no single uncontested interpretation of what it meant. It was generally taken to signify the process through which one becomes a cultivated and educated person, a person who is knowledgeable and who has good taste, but whereas many took *Bildung* to be synonymous with the acquisition of Enlightenment ideas, or even with the process through which one becomes sympathetic to the French Revolution, others took it to mean the formation of a proper religious disposition. Many also thought that an educated, cultivated person had a responsibility to enlighten a broad public through writings that addressed social, cultural, and political issues; this aspect of *Bildung* certainly informed Hegel's early career aspirations to become a public intellectual. And the person of *Bildung* acquired the authority and responsibility of a public intellectual not by way of birth or aristocratic title, but on account of the knowledge and character expressed by anyone who would succeed in the project of self-formation.

There is a general shape to the process of *Bildung* for Hegel, which echoes the way he sees other problems work themselves out dialectically: it is typically the movement from a stage of immediate unity, immersion, and harmony, through a stage of difference, deflection, and alienation, and then finally achieving a state of reconciliation (which is not as straightforward as 'thesis-antithesis-synthesis,' the typical oversimplification of his view). The final stage is not a return to the harmony and unity of the first stage, nor is it any kind of flat denial of the second moment; it is supposed to be a kind of acceptance and affirmation coupled with a genuine solution to the tensions of the second moment that prevents those tensions from dominating or destroying an individual or group. There is also the strong implication that the stage of reconciliation better satisfies the now educated aims of the individual or group. In the process, the aims themselves are developed and not identical to the initially inchoate or misdirected aims; the aspirations of the initial state in most cases either cannot be satisfied, or can only be satisfied at great cost. From the point of view of reconciliation, the initial aims will seem naïve, misguided and false, and the attempt to return to and take up those initial desires will be ironic.

iv. PLAN AND STRATEGY OF THE BOOK

In what follows, I have tried to remain attentive to the needs of those who are reading Hegel for the first time, including those who are new to philosophy as a discipline. With this in mind, I have avoided the various scholarly and exegetical arguments connected with the texts I am considering, not because they are uninteresting, but because engaging them would force me to use a much more technical vocabulary, and would also require a much longer book to address them satisfactorily. I have also tried to focus on those of Hegel's writings that are most often anthologized and used as texts in university-level courses. This book does not develop a critical view of Hegel's project, and, if anything, errs on the side of being too sympathetic; but readers of this book, I take it, are more in need of a clear understanding of Hegel's philosophy on its own terms, which is anyway a prerequisite for serious criticism. I might add that I have also avoided Hegel's obscure language, even to the extent of avoiding quotation almost entirely. My reasoning here is based on years of teaching Hegel to undergraduate students, during which time I have realized that students benefit greatly from hearing Hegel's arguments in 'ordinary' language. I have found that students acquire a level of confidence from this that helps them return to and struggle with Hegel's text.

This introductory chapter provides the historical and thematic groundwork to start reading Hegel's own texts. The next chapter, Chapter 2, is concerned with all of Hegel's writings prior to the publication of his first major work, the *Phenomenology of Spirit* (1807). In his early writings, Hegel is primarily concerned with the question of how to overcome the tensions and oppositions of modern life, and he considers at various points whether love, religion, or reason, will provide the best sort of reconciliation.

Chapter 3 considers the *Phenomenology of Spirit*, especially the basic theme of supersession, where one mode of consciousness or life gives way to another, and this latter mode is superior, either because it resolves tensions inherent in the prior stage, or because it is generally more stable or satisfying. The *Phenomenology* tries to capture this development from the point of view of consciousness, faced with various existential and epistemological crises, which stand to be answered in more or less satisfying ways. This chapter also explains the overall movement of the *Phenomenology*, and the important idea of mutual intersubjective recognition.

Chapter 4 explains and demystifies Hegel's 'system,' paying particular attention to its presentation in his *Encyclopedia of the Philosophical Sciences*. Hegel is concerned to explain the structure of what is, but not from the point of view of consciousness or experience. Of particular interest here is his conception of 'the understanding' contrasted with 'reason,' and the structure of necessity in nature. It is important for Hegel that we understand the structure of reality so that we can see ourselves in it, as opposed to being somehow over and above, or fighting against it.

Hegel's main work of political philosophy is the *Philosophy of Right*, and Chapter 5 looks closely at his theory of freedom in that work. Major interpretive questions about his political philosophy are answered when the *Philosophy of Right* is considered in light of the other books addressed in earlier chapters. This chapter also shows how some of Hegel's early concerns are now addressed in his mature philosophy.

Chapter 6 considers Hegel's view of history, drawing mainly on his *Philosophy of History* and to some extent his *Lectures on the History of Philosophy*. In these works, Hegel is concerned to show that there is a kind of reason or structure to history; history is not, in his view, just one thing after another. The basic narrative of history, says Hegel, is the development and realization of freedom, which is supported by a succession of political arrangements and states. He makes the distinction between empirical history, what actually happens, and philosophical history, which is the deeper structural development that lies behind empirical history; this distinction is the key to understanding his comments about the 'end of history.'

Finally, the highest forms of reflection that Hegel calls 'absolute spirit,' are considered in Chapter 7. These are the practices of art, religion, and philosophy, each of which represents humanity's reflection on its most basic concerns and interests. Art shows us something about the ultimate structure of reality through sensuous objects, religion represents the same thing to us symbolically and metaphorically, and philosophy expresses the same in pure concepts. This final chapter explores these domains of 'absolute spirit' with special attention to the relationship between these types of reflection and the modern state.

CHAPTER 2

HEGEL'S EARLY WRITINGS: OVERCOMING SEPARATION

If we look more closely at the particular form worn by a philosophy we see that it arises, on the one hand, from the living original-
ity of the spirit whose work and spontaneity have re-established
and shaped the harmony that has been rent; and on the other
hand, from the particular form of the dichotomy from which
the system emerges. Dichotomy is the source of *the need for
philosophy*; and as the culture of the era, it is the unfree and given
aspect of the whole configuration. (D 89)

In recent decades, the consumption of various human enhancement
technologies has increased at a staggering rate, especially the use
of drugs for treating depression, anxiety, and other such conditions,
but also the surgical manipulation of our bodies to conform to cultural standards of attractiveness. Americans are the most aggressive
consumers in this domain, but the phenomenon seems to have
already spread to other parts of the world as well. Even if we allow
that some people have pressing and legitimate needs for these
technologies, we are still left with the vast majority of consumers
who seem to be utilizing these technologies for other reasons; and
since these technologies have emerged so forcefully as part of a
broad cultural trend, it is worth asking whether there might be an
explanation that has traction at this level. There is certainly an
ongoing debate about whether these technologies have become a
way of life for us, and whether consumers are mainly interested in
happiness, success, authenticity, or just the alleviation of boredom;

there is also debate about whether these chemicals and procedures actually make anyone happier, more successful or authentic, or even less likely to suffer from boredom. And of course, part of the explanation will require attention to how these technologies are marketed, how they play into the various economic incentives at work, and whether consumers are manipulated or misinformed in any way.

But another way to approach this trend is to consider whether we are just reaching for these technologies to alleviate the general malaise of our modern predicament. On this view, it is not so much that we have specific reasons for consuming these technologies, or even particular goals that we are trying to attain through them; rather, we are just reacting to some very basic features of modernity, specifically the way modernity has taken shape in contemporary Western, industrialized, and technologically advanced democracies. In this setting, we typically enjoy more basic legal and political freedoms than previous generations, but we wear these hard-won freedoms uncomfortably and with great ambivalence. More freedom means more choices, but then, it also means more anxiety about what to choose; it may mean that we have more projects and possibilities, but then also more potential conflict between overlapping obligations and interests. Our modern freedom is partially expressed by our enhanced ability and willingness to question and criticize, but then, this same critical rationality that freed us from past oppressions may now become a source of torment and dissatisfaction: as we slide towards cynicism and ironic detachment, it becomes increasingly difficult to identify with the institutions and politics of modern society, since we can so easily spot the vagaries of bureaucracy and the corruption and venality of politics. And when we momentarily overcome our cynicism and try to engage the institutional structures of our society, we are often frustrated by the sheer complexity and opacity of our modern world. In the face of these modern malaises, then, one is likely to feel disempowered and vaguely anxious, which makes it all too easy to reach for a quick technological fix.

Hegel lived long before our contemporary enhancement technologies came on the scene, of course, but his solution to the problems of modernity may well turn out to be much more effective than ours; for Hegel, the solution is philosophy. The proffered solutions of his day were various forms of religion and mysticism, romanticism about the past, and a number of political responses that tended to boil down to oppression and authoritarianism. But Hegel urged us to follow our critical rationality through to its natural end: philosophy can help us reconcile the contradictions that emerge in our lives by using reason to see through these oppositions and dichotomies. Philosophy cannot make these tensions disappear entirely, but it can cultivate the sort of understanding that reconciles us to our world, and encourages us to start asking the right questions about it; and these are prerequisites, Hegel thinks, for then changing our world in lasting and satisfying ways.

The main reason Hegel's early writings are important is that they show us how deeply pragmatic, engaged, and worldly his project is. He was deeply moved by the cross-currents of European culture at the end of the eighteenth century, and tried to find a way to overcome the many forms of separation that had emerged. He was convinced that a kind of unity and harmony could exist in modern life, but only as a 'unity in difference,' as he put it. He sought a synthesis of the Enlightenment and romanticism, reason and faith, individual and society. And he knew that this synthesis could not be the easy result of intellectual intuition or inarticulate emotion; it had to be a unity with an internal structure and, in his early works, he began to conceptualize this structure as reason, as reason manifest in the world. Hegel's early writings reveal the ideals that would stay with him for the rest of his career, and offer students of Hegel the best interpretive guide for making sense of his overall project.

Hegel's 'early writings' are usually taken to include everything he wrote prior to the *Phenomenology of Spirit*, which was published in 1807, so this includes the material he wrote while living in Berne (1793–97), Frankfurt (1797–1800), and Jena (1801–07). His first published work appeared in 1801, titled *The Difference between Fichte's and Schelling's Systems of Philosophy* (now typically referred to as the *Differenzschrift*, or the '*Difference* essay'), just after he moved to Jena, and around the time that he began work as a private tutor and as co-editor with Schelling of the *Critical*

Journal of Philosophy. Other writings from before the *Difference* essay were not published in Hegel's lifetime, and only came to the attention of Hegel scholars in the early twentieth century. These exist mainly as fragments, and have come to be referred to as *The Earliest System-Programme of German Idealism* (1796–97), *Love* (1797–98), and *Fragment of a System* (Frankfurt, 1800). Around the same time that he was working on the *Difference* essay, Hegel was also pre-occupied with political issues, in an unpublished essay titled *The German Constitution* (1797–1801), and an essay that was published with the title *Natural Law* (1802–03).

There are also a number of essays and fragments that concern religion, Christianity in particular. The manuscript titled *The Positivity of the Christian Religion* (referred to as the '*Positivity* essay') was originally written while Hegel was in Berne, and though he continued to work on it while in Frankfurt, it was never published. Hegel worked on his essay *The Life of Jesus* (1795) while in Berne, and on *The Spirit of Christianity and its Fate* (1799), a partial revision of the *Positivity* essay, while in Frankfurt. And while Hegel was living in Jena, he published an essay titled *Faith and Knowledge*.

We find in these early works Hegel's first efforts to overcome the main forms of separation that characterized the modern world: (i) redefining the nature of 'reason' in the course of criticizing Kant, and with an eye towards grasping the whole, which he refers to as 'the absolute'; (ii) developing a theory of love, which lays the groundwork for his seminal ideas about mutual recognition; (iii) articulating a powerful critique of Christianity that will later inform his analysis of the 'unhappy consciousness' in the *Phenomenology*, and from which his notion of 'spirit' emerges; and (iv) laying out an analysis of 'spirit' and culture that both identifies the structural challenges of modern society and sets the agenda for a distinctively modern conception of 'ethical life.'

i. THE NEED FOR PHILOSOPHY

At the turn of the century, Hegel is working to understand and realize an ideal of unity, wholeness, and completeness. He shares this ideal of unity, as well as the practice of referring to it as 'the absolute,' with Hölderlin and Schelling, and expresses it in a way that draws on both romantic and Enlightenment influences. This ideal emerged as a response to the cultural and political currents in Europe that seemed to sever a number of longstanding connections between humanity and the world. Modern technology had changed our thinking about nature, from something in which we were deeply and inextricably embedded, to something that we could control and harness for our own purposes. Religious ideologies had been questioned and challenged, and no longer functioned as the absolute guide for human conduct and affairs. The idea of individual rights relative to state power had strengthened the sense that human beings exist first and foremost as individuals, without already having ties to others.

Each of these cultural currents was of course immensely empowering for people, since it was at least in principle possible for people to make their own decisions and live their own lives without the arbitrary interference of nature, or the arbitrary authority of religion or politics, getting in the way. But at the same time, these sweeping cultural changes were also alienating, because they meant that we had moved away from traditional sources of meaning without any clear indication of whether they needed to be replaced, and if so, what sort of replacement would be possible or desirable.

Responding to this loss of traditional sources of meaning, and to the general sense that the world had become disenchanted, Hölderlin and other romantic poets and writers explored metaphors of unity and wholeness. We must overcome our separation from nature, they suggested, by embracing it in a new way, by refashioning our language in a way that unifies humanity ('spirit') and nature. If traditional forms of religion have fallen under Enlightenment scrutiny, leaving behind a secular world of merely human affairs, then we must spiritualize or divinize our world in a new way. And if modern politics separates us from each other by treating us as a collection of isolated atoms, then we must turn to traditional forms of community and togetherness to preserve our human ties to each other. Romantics would argue that the solution for all of these forms of separation is to be found in poetry and the arts, folk religion, culture, intuition, and passion. In fact, most romantics at the time were heavily invested in polemical exchanges with Enlightenment thinkers, in which they positioned themselves against rationality, intellectualism, and philosophy.

It must be understood, though, that this opposition between romanticism and the Enlightenment is easily exaggerated; it would be better to think of these seemingly antagonistic currents as obverse sides of the same coin. It may be granted that each took hold in Europe at different times and locations, and that each was susceptible to overblown rhetoric, but overall, they are both part of the modern European self-understanding of modernity. Hegel certainly channels both of these currents in his philosophy, and is interested in the sort of self-correcting dynamic that might emerge from this antagonistic and ambivalent European response to the separation, fragmentation, and alienation of modern life. But Hegel does state his allegiance to the rationalism of the Enlightenment in a rather definitive way, even early in his career. Along with Schelling, Hegel thought that the ideal of unity was essential to human reason, and that philosophy should seek a kind of unity and wholeness in reason; but since Hegel was not simply siding with rationalism over romanticism, he needed to redefine reason, against its traditional formulation, so that it could capture this unity.

Rethinking the nature of reason such that it can express this unity is Hegel's project in the *Difference* essay especially, but also to some extent in *The Earliest System-Programme, Love,* and *Fragment of a System*. For Hegel, no philosophy can be genuinely systematic if it falls short of expressing this unity. Kant aspired to make his philosophy systematic, but it appeared to fall well short of that goal as Hegel and others redefined the criteria of systematicity to include this new thinking and theorizing of the whole. Hegel's generation was anyway rightly preoccupied with the question of what to do with the post-Kantian project, since Kant left them with a number of unsatisfying and unsystematic dichotomies: phenomena and 'noumena,' freedom and necessity, subjectivity and objectivity, reason and faith, and mind and body. In the *Difference* essay, Hegel writes about Schelling's and Fichte's attempts to complete Kant's system, to discern the next step in the post-Kantian project. The primary dichotomy in this context is between realism and idealism, and

Hegel argues that there is no way out of the debate between realists and idealists so long as the only recognized moves are those that locate a first principle in one side of the dichotomy or the other (either realism against idealism, or idealism against realism).

The problem with Kant's philosophy, Hegel argues, is that it never quite gets beyond 'the understanding' (*Verstand*) to explore the possible syntheses of 'reason' (*Vernunft*). These are terms of art for Hegel, and he distinguishes them in the following way: the former signifies our capacity to carve up reality into manageable parts, to make distinctions and think abstractly, while the latter signifies the ability to grasp the whole as a totality, which requires the move beyond oppositions and dichotomies. Hegel is clear, though, that 'the understanding' carries out necessary and useful work: we need to make distinctions so that we can comprehend what is going on the world, and grasping reality in this way is a positive and creative act. Indeed, without 'the understanding,' we would be left only with mysticism, superstition, and a rather paltry grasp of reality. But we should not stop after 'the understanding' has done its work, because we then run the risk of suffering at the hands of our own creation: the basic dichotomies of 'the understanding' tend to outlive their usefulness as they become ossified by cultural practices and institutions, and ultimately undermine the unity of life.

Hegel also argues that the need for philosophy will naturally and immanently arise in developed societies, and this may be among the most interesting parts of the *Difference* essay. This happens because the intellectual aptitudes required for the development of any society will largely be facets of 'the understanding,' which will produce any number of distinctions that will then tend towards ossification and rigidity. These societies will then slide towards frustration as they attempt to understand themselves and the world with these rigid distinctions, always failing to grasp the organic whole, always tending towards impasse. As these frustrations evolve into ruptures and a whole culture becomes disjointed, Hegel thinks, it will be philosophy that has the tools for dealing with it. Philosophy based on 'reason' in addition to 'the understanding' can reveal the unity, the living connection behind apparent oppositions, and generate new formulations of the basic questions that a society takes to be fundamental.

It is worth noting that Hegel is not at all advocating a class of philosopher-kings who claim complete knowledge of reality, and who disseminate their findings to an otherwise hapless public. All Hegel assumes is that societies will tend to have a set of basic concerns and interests, and that their pursuit of these will recruit some sort of collective self-understanding and comprehension of the world. These societies will of necessity employ language, concepts, distinctions, and such, in the practice of collective reflection, and if these distinctions become rigid, they will fix the way questions are framed, their sense of possibilities for the future, and so on. Philosophy, according to Hegel, is particularly good at articulating whatever it is that matters most to a society, locating those dichotomies that lie at the center of a society's sense of itself, and, in the face of major ruptures, reframing the basic values and questions with an eye towards the whole, 'the absolute.'

In the case of the post-Kantian project, the typical moves had been to fix one side of the subjective-objective split and work from there; but Hegel was interested in whatever point of view could appropriate both the subjective and the objective equally. Since Hegel thought that Kant's philosophy was essentially tied to European culture and the emerging currents of modernity, whatever unity could be found at the level of 'reason' regarding Kant's philosophy would be tightly connected to the unity that, by hypothesis, resolves the oppositions of European culture.

These are ambitious claims on behalf of philosophy, and Hegel was formulating them long before he knew exactly how to substantiate them; but he did seem to be asking the right questions, and these questions would continue to preoccupy him throughout his career. If 'reason' seeks unity behind opposition, is that unity somehow already there waiting to be discovered? Or is the unity something that is produced by reason? And how are we supposed to talk about 'the whole' and 'totality' without slipping back into distinctions and the language of 'the understanding'? How do we show that 'reason' on this formulation is not just a new version of mysticism?

ii. LOVE AND RECOGNITION

Kant's philosophy did not offer any way to reconcile or unify the basic opposition between subject and object, knower and world. As Hegel first started to fashion his own solution to this problem, he was guided by two main ideas: the first was Schelling's argument that the only way forward was through a philosophy of nature, which would then transcend the opposition of subject and object by subsuming both in the processes of organic development; the second was Hölderlin's argument that Fichte's view is too radically subjectivist, and his claim that the only way past the opposition of subject and object is to start with the assumption of a community of knowers who all experience a shared world.

Hegel starts to bring these ideas together in his unpublished fragment on *Love*, which describes the sort of unity that can exist between two people who love each other, an analogue for the unity of subject and object. He then modifies and develops this framework in *Natural Law* and the *System of Ethical Life*, hoping to accommodate more general epistemological, ethical, and political concerns. It is here that Hegel begins speaking of mutual intersubjective recognition, 'spirit,' and 'ethical life,' ideas that will be central to the *Phenomenology* as well as his mature thought.

In a genuinely loving relationship, Hegel argues, we find a kind of subject-object unity because each person will see himself or herself in the other, and each will embrace this, even though it is a kind of dependence or constraint. When one loves another person, one will, to some extent, adopt the other's interests and projects as one's own; this is an expansion of self, but one that carries with it an increase in vulnerability. The lover (the subject) and the loved (the object) will form a unity, which will recursively condition how each thinks about 'self' and 'other' in this context.

But, according to Hegel, the unity of love also contains moments of disunity and difference: lovers have physically distinct bodies, separate (and at least partially inscrutable) minds, and unique personal histories. And since lovers are human, they are mortal, which guarantees a final and irrevocable independence; no one can share the experience of another's death, nor can any unity exist between a living and a dead thing. Hegel thinks that this explains why love always seems to be grasping for the eternal, to resist this last stubborn element of independence. Interestingly, Hegel thinks that the existence of children has a special status in light of these considerations: when a child is born, it is the expression of its parents' unity, which cannot itself be dissolved, since it is now a single thing.

Notice that in this analysis of love, Hegel is already attempting to show that a unity, identity, or totality, need not be a blank or gratuitous reference; there is a structure to love, a dynamic structure of mediation that brings two people into a functional unity, and allows for each continually to renegotiate the bounds of selfhood. The structure, or rationality, of love will have phases of 'immature' and 'mature' unity, dynamics of dependence and independence, and moments of self-sacrifice and surrender, as well as self-development and empowerment. Love involves two human beings, but the complex structure of love will bring them together as a single organism.

Hegel is talking specifically about relationships of love in modernity, so he is assuming that by the time anyone is in a relationship of love, she or he has internalized the distinctions that shape the ideologies, institutions, politics, and ambitions of our world. For example, Hegel argues that the institution of private property separates us from each other because it artificially emphasizes individuality, and if this is too deeply or rigidly internalized, such that people in a relationship continue to think of their possessions and their bodies as private property, love may not be possible. Possession and property rights are of course entrenched features of the modern world, but wherever love is possible, it rediscovers life, because at least in the context of the relationship, all distinctions become ironic and are seen as partial and illusory. To the extent that love gives us a taste of the world taken as a whole, it teaches us something fundamental about reality; Hegel even claims that love 'completely destroys objectivity' (L 31).

In the *Natural Law* essay, Hegel engages the debate about the foundation of natural rights, and argues that neither transcendental theories (Kant and Fichte) nor empiricist theories (Hobbes and Locke) have it right. Both theories fail, Hegel says, because they lack the conceptual resources to talk about society as a whole; they begin with a number of presuppositions about individuals as bearers of rights, and remain trapped by this individualist prejudice, unable to describe how our highest human interests and deepest normative structures are embedded in cultures taken as wholes, irreducible to the individuals who comprise them. Hegel insists that we must employ the ideas of 'spirit' and 'ethical life' if we are to properly understand the nature of rights, and so also, culture, normativity, modernity, and so on.

Hegel had briefly explored the possibility that love was the key to overcoming atomism and grasping the whole, but in the years leading up to the *Phenomenology of Spirit*, he shifted emphasis away from love. Love may not be the perfect overcoming of the opposition between subject and object, Hegel thought, since love may be too deeply entrenched in our natural desires, and since no relationship between a man and a woman could be truly equal so long as it existed in a world characterized by radical gender inequality (as nineteenth-century Europe certainly was). He would continue to think that love in the context of one's private life is essential for self-development, but in the drafts that would lead to the *Phenomenology*, Hegel re-describes the basic connection we have to other human beings in terms of inter-subjective recognition.

Although the definitive account of recognition appears in the *Phenomenology*, its basic structure is already becoming clear in the drafts leading up to that work, where Hegel distinguishes between the sort of recognition that might occur between persons who are free and equal (what you might call 'pure' or 'mutual' recognition) and the recognition that occurs between persons who are unequal in some respect ('impure' recognition, what Hegel calls later the 'master-slave' dialectic). He also explores the way that relations of recognition can be solidified in the public sphere, through institutionalization and law. It is also in these pre-*Phenomenology* writings that Hegel begins to formulate his conception of 'ethical life,' which signifies the totality of relations of recognition in a society. It is in and through the relations of 'ethical life' that each and every person becomes free and follows a path of self-development. Hegel's notion of 'ethical life' will be developed in the *Phenomenology*, and then become the central form of unity-in-difference for his political philosophy in the *Philosophy of Right*, but at this point, it should just be noted that with this idea, Hegel definitively moves away from Kant. Recall that Kant's ethical theory is based on claims that are universal, ahistorical, and detached from the particularities of culture; Hegel's conception of 'ethical life' places history, politics, and culture at the center of our thinking about ethics.

iii. GOD HIMSELF IS DEAD

Many of Hegel's early writings are about religion, and this is unsurprising given the time he spent at the seminary, his interest in the philosophical problems of religion, and his concern with religion as an entrenched feature of modern European culture. Hegel's view of Christianity in particular is complex and subtle, and his commitments in this regard are elusive at best; any interpretation of how Christianity fits into his philosophy will have to account for his highly unorthodox use of terms like 'God,' 'spirit,' and 'the divine,' as well as a number of inconsistent comments about Christianity across his published and unpublished writings, lectures, and letters. But many of Hegel's readers, then and now, want desperately to know whether he is properly described as a Christian, or rather as a pantheist, or a humanist, or even as an atheist. In fact, it was precisely this dispute among Hegel's followers in the nineteenth Century that led to a major split, between those who thought of him as an essentially Christian philosopher with conservative politics (the so-called 'right Hegelians') and those who read him as an atheist and humanist with radical politics (the so-called 'left Hegelians'); though some matters in this regard have been settled over the past century of scholarly work on Hegel, the issue is still a live one for many commentators.

But the early writings taken as a whole are deeply critical of Christianity, anticipating what Ludwig Feuerbach, Karl Marx, and even Friedrich Nietzsche will say about Christianity years later, and the key critical points of these early writings will stay with Hegel throughout his career. It is worth pointing out in that regard that Hegel (not Nietzsche) should get credit for first announcing the death of God; Hegel argues in the *Phenomenology*, that after Jesus' crucifixion, 'God himself is dead' (PHG § 785), because without the mediation between God and humanity that the figure of Jesus provided, humanity will suffer separation, alienation, and despair. Of course, Hegel will argue years later, in his *Lectures on the Philosophy of Religion* (delivered four times while living in Berlin, from 1821–31), and in the third part of his *Encyclopedia* (the *Philosophy of Mind*), that modern Christianity does in fact capture some part of the truth of the world, and that it does this more effectively than any other modern religion; but the critical points remain, and for this reason, it would be flatly wrong to characterize him as an orthodox Christian philosopher, and misleading to describe him even as a Christian philosopher, since his ideas are incompatible with most forms of Christianity today. Whether Hegel also has substantive commitments to pantheism, humanism, or atheism is another question, one best raised in the light of his mature work.

But if we are just looking at the early writings on religion, we will need to consider: *The Life of Jesus* (written while in Bern, 1795, but never published), *The Positivity of the Christian Religion* (written in Bern, revised in Frankfurt, but never published), *The Spirit of Christianity and its Fate* (written in Frankfurt, 1799, but not published), and *Faith and Knowledge* (written while living in Jena, and published in 1802). In *The Life of Jesus*, Hegel argues (anachronistically) that the rational core of what Jesus taught is Kantian ethics: true virtue is acquired by acting freely and rationally, by autonomously subjecting oneself to the demands of moral law. But, Hegel argues, in the early stages of Christianity, this rational core was lost, and supplanted by a form of authoritarianism. This corruption of Jesus' proto-Kantianism was due largely to historical conditions, to the limitations on what most people at the time could understand, and how this shaped those early efforts to spread the religion. The tendency of early Christianity, Hegel suggests, was to idolize the person of Jesus, focusing on the inherent authority of his words and his person, instead of on the authority of the rational principles he endorsed.

At this point in Hegel's development, he very much agreed with the spirit of Kant's ethics, and wanted to preserve Kant's rationalistic conception of human dignity: it is because we are free and rational creatures that we have a special moral standing in the world. But Kant had already moved away from orthodox Christianity, defending an 'intellectualist' conception of God's will, according to which human rationality is a reflection of God's own image, and must be cultivated by each of us so that we can understand and embrace moral law. In the debates of the eighteenth century, this 'intellectualist' view would be contrasted with a 'voluntarist' view, which holds that God's will, by its own inherent authority, is morally right. According to Hegel's interpretation, then, Jesus was actually a rationalist philosopher with an 'intellectualist' conception of God's will: the moral law (the presumptive will of God) was knowable to us through reason, and binding for us through self-legislation (not by way of God's command).

Christianity, then, according to Hegel, could have expressed its rational core, but instead of asserting its authority on the basis of reason, it rather turned to other sources of authority like the charismatic figure of Jesus, the will of God, miracles, dogma, ritual, and whatever legal and political institutions enforce compliance with religious rules. The extent to which Christianity appealed to these extra-rational and arbitrary sources of authority is the extent to which Christianity became 'positive.' When early Christians acted in accordance with this authoritarianism, this 'positivity,' they were acting, as Kant would put it, 'heteronomously' instead of autonomously; and for Kant, 'heteronomous' actions have no moral worth. But Hegel does not think that early Christians as individuals are to be blamed for this; rather, he thinks that authoritarianism was necessary at the time, because people had become enfeebled and receptive to domination as a result of the collapse of the Greek and Roman states.

In the *Positivity* essay, Hegel takes it as obvious that Christianity had in fact become 'positive,' and pursued the question whether, despite its positivity, Christianity could become a genuine 'people's religion.' Hegel's model for a 'people's religion' was ancient Greece, which was characterized by a this-worldly religion virtually indistinguishable from politics and the state; a genuine civic religion acknowledges no distinction between individual and collective salvation, personal and civic virtue, or private and public goods.

A modern civic religion has these features, but is also based on reason, which would be expressed through all levels of social organization. But Christianity, according to Hegel, is far too preoccupied with narratives of personal salvation, and fills people's heads with superstitions that draw their attention towards the other-worldly; the result of this is that people become politically detached and ignorant of their own society's history. And this is just what happened during the Roman Empire, Hegel says, as people became increasingly concerned with their own private, individual affairs, preoccupied with fear of death, and politically unengaged. This political detachment left them much more easily manipulated and ready to accept authority, and their fear of death made them ready to accept superstitious claims about the afterlife.

But in the *Life of Jesus* and the *Positivity* essay, Hegel's argument is not merely that Christianity has abandoned its rational principles; he argues that Christian teachings actually undermine and compete with virtue, and he brings this out by comparing Jesus with Socrates. Hegel's view is that Socrates, the champion of reason, would be the ideal leader of a civic religion, as opposed to Jesus, the champion of authority; the former empowered people by teaching them to embrace rationality and free thinking, while the latter infantilized people by teaching them to accept arbitrary sources of authority. But it was not at all clear to Hegel that Christianity could be reformed or replaced; its authoritarianism permeated all of its practices, and its place in European culture seemed far too entrenched.

Accordingly, in *The Spirit of Christianity and its Fate*, Hegel accepts that Christianity is here to stay for the foreseeable future, not because it ever had better arguments than paganism, but because of a number of historical accidents that fueled its cultural entrenchment. So he now takes up a more traditional and less anachronistic interpretation of Jesus as a teacher of love, not reason. Hegel makes similar arguments in this work as in the fragment on *Love*, but here the teachings of love are attributed to Jesus, and the content of love is described in terms of faith. *The Spirit of Christianity* is the only place where Hegel suggests that love and faith might be higher than reason, and also the only context where reason steps aside for the sake of mysticism. It is because of these claims that Hegel seems to have changed his mind about Christianity; but regardless of the precise meaning of *The Spirit of Christianity*, it clearly stands out as an oddity relative to all of his other writings. The mysticism that Hegel seems to embrace here was a startling reversal at the time, and it was quickly abandoned, never to resurface again. The best explanation of this momentary reversal might be that it was an experiment of his emerging speculative hermeneutics. Recall that his speculative hermeneutics requires a form of sympathetic interpretation that, when a social practice is its object, takes account of the internal point of view of the participants to discern its point or end. After realizing that Christianity was too entrenched to be reformed or removed, Hegel tried to find 'the rational in the real,' not through the 'external' critique laid out in *The Life of Jesus*, but now by taking up the point of view of practicing Christians. But when he did this, he ended up anticipating an argument about authority and infantilization that will later appear in *Phenomenology*; and this argument, which leads to a characterization of what Hegel calls 'the unhappy consciousness,' is at least as harshly critical of Christianity as anything in the *Positivity* essay (PHG §§ 207–23). The 'unhappy consciousness' emerges as a result of the separation between humanity and God, where the former is taken to be finite, imperfect, powerless, and mortal, and the latter is taken to be infinite, perfect, omnipotent, and immortal. As Christians internalize this opposition, they tend to slide into self-loathing, since after all, the opposition suggests to them that their lives are really quite pathetic compared to God's. As their estimation of themselves spirals downward, the urge to identify with and yearn for the perfections of the divine is intensified; this urge is typically manifested by devotional thought and action, self-sacrifice on behalf of the divine, and so on. Over time, the internal struggle of the 'unhappy consciousness' leads to the total denial of self and the inability to use reason and critical reflection for the purposes of self-empowerment. At this point, the religious believer is easily subjugated and manipulated by earthly powers, especially those who present themselves as divine.

In the last of the early writings on religion, *Faith and Knowledge*, Hegel brings together the arguments he made in the *Difference* essay with his assessment of the nature of culture and the modern state. *Faith and Knowledge* is primarily a criticism of the philosophies of Kant, Jacobi, and Fichte, but what may be more interesting than the detailed criticism is the general way that Hegel situates the problem: European culture at the beginning of the nineteenth century is characterized by a fundamental opposition between the other-worldliness of Christianity and the this-worldliness of the scientific worldview characteristic of the Enlightenment, and it is precisely this rupture that gets recapitulated in the philosophical systems of the day. This rupture, then, is an example of what Hegel was imagining in the *Difference* essay, that dichotomies will take root and ossify in a culture and will cause all sorts of havoc, unless a philosophy that employs 'reason' instead of just 'the understanding' can help people see things differently.

iv. ALIENATION, COMMUNITY, AND THE MODERN STATE

We have seen in these early writings that Hegel responds to the separation, fragmentation, and alienation of modern life by first calling on philosophy to diagnose the structural features of our modern world, especially where they seem to generate oppositions and even ruptures. Some of these oppositions appear clearly in Kant's philosophy, for example, between phenomena and 'noumena,' and between freedom and necessity, but Hegel thinks that the same oppositions will have broad cultural manifestations as well. The most basic popular manifestation is between the values of the Enlightenment and the values of religion, between reason and faith. We have also seen that Hegel considers the potential remedies of love, religion, and mysticism, but then rejects these as he begins to formulate his own distinctive ideas. And his nascent conceptions of reason, inter-subjective recognition, 'spirit,' and 'ethical life' emerge during this period as he thinks about the fundamental questions at hand. How are individuals supposed to integrate their own interests and projects with those of others? What is the basic connection between 'spirit' and culture? How is 'ethical life' to be analyzed in terms of reason? And can these concerns be addressed by the modern state?

Hegel had been thinking about the problems of modern culture, and about whether any modern state could effectively deal with these problems since at least 1797, when he began work on an essay titled *The German Constitution*. Although the essay is centrally concerned with political and military issues surrounding France's expansion (which, at this time, came to absorb the city of Mainz), and although Hegel never had the essay published, it nonetheless contains a few important philosophical points about the nature of the modern state and about the relationship between 'culture,' 'spirit,' and 'ethical life.' When placed alongside his other pre-*Phenomenology* writings, it is clear that Hegel had already developed much of his account of the systemic dissatisfactions of modern culture as well as the forms of 'spirit' that emerge in light of this. Specifically, he argued that Germany fell short of being a true state, because it did not embrace a commonly shared project with which each and every citizen could identify, and because it did not support a complex institutional structure that would make freedom possible for its citizens. A true state, Hegel urged, must defend individual rights, bind itself to a constitution and the rule of law, and have democratic representation.

In the years after *The German Constitution*, while working on the drafts of the *Phenomenology*, Hegel continued to think about the overall form of the modern state, especially where alienation is generated from the tension between the universality of Enlightenment ideals and the particularity of typical small town life, culture, and religion. He was also concerned about the influence of the free market, how it was needed to secure individual freedoms, but also dangerous because the wealth and poverty that would inevitably be created would undermine the rule of law. Hegel thought that the modern European culture of that time was characterized by the deeply embedded opposition between reason and faith, and he thought that the German state was powerless to address this rupture. It was not clear at all how *Bildung* could acculturate people properly in these conditions, and it seemed likely that any *Bildung* that could then be in effect would only serve to reproduce these ruptures. The philosophical reconciliation of these basic ruptures of culture would be a prerequisite for *Bildung* to function properly, but it may be that only the cultivated (*gebildete*) few are in a position to effect this reconciliation in the first place.

Before considering the paradoxical difficulties of a ruptured culture, though, we should understand Hegel's view of alienation and how it might be overcome in an idealized 'ethical life' based on a sphere of culture without major oppositions. First of all, the term 'alienation' collapses a distinction that exists in German, between *Entfremdung* and *Entäusserung*. These can both be translated as 'alienation,' but whereas the former suggests distance, strangeness, and separation between oneself and one's world, the latter suggests a kind of intentional or deliberate surrender or relinquishment. The latter sense best captures the essential dynamic of *Bildung*; in fact, one can understand the process of *Bildung* as that through which one remedies the ills of alienation (*Entfremdung*) through alienation (*Entäusserung*). In this context, what must be 'surrendered' is one's atomistic self-understanding, the state in which one imagines a fundamental separation from other people and from the society and culture in which one lives. In Hegel's view, the more one can make one's actions and ends intelligible in terms of the wider structured context that mediates them, the more one feels integrated in 'ethical life.' If one cannot see how one's actions and ends can fit into the world at the same time that they can be 'one's own,' then one will experience alienation in the sense of *Entfremdung*. But if the ideal of 'ethical life' is to be realized, individuals must be able to see their actions as their own and at the same time be able to identify with publicly shared goals that express some unity at the level of society as a whole.

Back in Berne, when he wrote *The Earliest System-Programme* (1796–97), Hegel seemed to think that a ruptured culture could not be reconciled by reason and philosophy alone: if humankind is to understand the world and its relation to the world, it must be propelled by a mythology of reason that also recruits the passions. Still heavily influenced by Hölderlin's romanticism and Schiller's *Letters*, Hegel imagined an aestheticized reason that generates a quasi-religious mythology, not one based on superstition or authoritarianism, but on reason. The spokespersons for this new mythology will be philosopher-poets who speak to both the enlightened and the unenlightened, and themselves become sensuous just as the people become more rational. Hegel also made this point in the fragment on *Love*, arguing that the unity-in-difference of love cannot be attained through the power of the understanding or reason alone; there must also be feelings, passion, and desire. Hegel's thinking at this point indicated that 'spirit' would emerge in a culture that had overcome its oppositions, and supported the development of whole and integrated human beings; an aestheticized mythology of reason would draw people through their comprehensive development and realize 'ethical life.'

But in the years just prior to the *Phenomenology*, it was clear that Hegel had abandoned this romantic notion. In the drafts leading up to that work, he had already started subordinating art and religion to philosophy, and thinking about the analysis of ruptured cultures in these terms. He needed an account of how individuals fashion strategies of identification in the world, one that captured the difficulties people face when they engage with the opaque, contingent, and complicated modern world. He started to think about alienation (*Entfremdung*) in terms of the inability to take up social identities that are connected with the public goods and interests of the whole. On this line of thought, merely collective activities, based on shared cultural and linguistic practices, are not sufficient for overcoming alienation; rather, one must be able to affirm an identity that is political, that has a more intelligible connection to the general good than one finds in merely collective activities. Hegel is now thinking of the process of *Bildung* that would manage these strategies as a mediated version of inter-subjective recognition. Specifically, the important normative feature of civil society is that individuals can come to recognize each other as full, free, and rational agents through the exchange of the market, and they share more substantive types of recognition in other institutions of civil society.

In these early writings, Hegel is asking more questions about the modern state and alienation than he has answers for, and he is still measuring how far he can push romantic ideals without undermining his more basic commitments to modernism and Enlightenment values. His political views will not fully settle for another decade or so, but at this point he is already thinking about 'ethical life' and 'spirit,' which puts him in dialogue with various debates in contemporary political philosophy about community, tolerance, neutrality, and pluralism. Hegel's political philosophy is often taken to include a strong notion of community, one that sounds premodern, or at least in conflict with today's liberal values; but this would be a serious misreading. In his main work of political philosophy, the *Philosophy of Right*, it is clear that Hegel is no 'communitarian,' but it is interesting to consider how, even in his earliest writings, he already reveals a set of commitments that are entirely incompatible with a strong notion of community.

In just these early writings, it is already clear that he is not interested in any conception of community that suppresses individual civil and political rights, nor could he accept any government not bound by the rule of law. As early as 1797, when he was working on *The German Constitution* and the fragment on *Love*, he is already thinking about community as a 'unity-in-difference.' Of course Hegel and others were modifying their political views in light of the French Revolution and its aftermath, but one constant in Hegel's thinking was the importance of individual rights. An embrace of individual rights was anyway over-determined for Hegel, since he could easily reach this position as a Kantian or as a romantic. He was thinking about the issue in terms of the 'organic state,' which may seem to imply a strong notion of community, but this was for Hegel a romantic political ideal, and his romanticism had always placed a supreme value on individual freedoms.

It should also be emphasized that when Hegel starts to analyze the relationship between self-sacrifice (*Entäusserung*) and alienation (*Entfremdung*), what is sacrificed is not individuality in general, let alone individual freedoms; what is to be surrendered is atomistic individualism that is based on an exceedingly narrow conception of self-interest. But again, his view is not fully developed at this point, and his intuitions about what counts for 'narrow' individualism have not settled; but when he frames the issue of alienation in modern culture, the problem he sees is that it is not clear how to have community and strong individual freedoms at the same time. He is not even considering the possibility of a stronger notion of community that would simply suppress individual freedom.

Finally, Hegel's early view of Christianity is relevant to the issue of community. Recall that his main criticism of Christianity is that it is authoritarian, in direct contradiction with the rational Kantian principles of freedom and autonomy. And recall also his argument in these early writings that anticipates the 'unhappy consciousness' argument in the *Phenomenology*; that argument aims to show that relating to a transcendent God, with all conceivable perfections, drives one towards the complete devaluation of one's own life and world. The disvalue of this 'unhappy consciousness,' in Hegel's view, is that it amounts to the destruction of individuality. Hegel's criticisms of Christianity, then, at least as they appear in these early writings, would apply just as well to the idea of community; if a strong community could be fairly described as authoritarian, then Hegel would have to reject it.

CHAPTER 3

THE *PHENOMENOLOGY OF SPIRIT*: THE SATISFACTIONS AND DISSATISFACTIONS OF CONSCIOUSNESS

Appearance is the arising and passing away that does not itself arise and pass away, but is 'in itself,' and constitutes the actuality and the movement of the life of truth. The True is thus the Bacchanalian revel in which no member is not drunk; yet because each member collapses as soon as he drops out, the revel is just as much transparent and simple repose. (PHG § 47)

In Fyodor Dostoyevsky's novel *Notes from the Underground* (1864), we are invited into the mind of an intelligent, yet seemingly disturbed, character who takes very seriously a number of philosophical questions about modernity, rationality, self-identity, consciousness, authenticity, moral psychology, freedom and responsibility. By his own description, he often spends months 'underground,' withdrawn from human affairs, because his interactions with others tend to be deeply unsatisfying. But then, his time underground become unsatisfying as well, and he is drawn to re-engage humanity, hoping against his better judgment that things will be different. A central feature of the Underground Man's self-understanding is his valorization of the free will, which he takes to be the essence of being human. But because he thinks that his will must be spontaneous and even capricious in order to express his true self, he becomes hyper-vigilant about any external influence that threatens to undermine the radical freedom of his will. Things spin out of control as he starts to question the spontaneity of his will, worrying that reason, science, passion, literature, and other people are all just so many threats to his humanity.

Dostoyevsky suggests (in a footnote) that the Underground Man represents a certain type of modern individual, a mode of consciousness, as it were, with its own contours and connections to the historical and cultural currents of the times. As the novel unfolds, we see the Underground Man on a trajectory of self-destruction and exhaustion, and notice that his overall pathology, his arrogance and insecurity, his inability to love another person, and so on, are all the logical products of his own mode of consciousness. His problems are not the result of external forces, but rather the internal structure of his self-understanding. It turns out that given his own criteria for satisfaction, coupled with his exceedingly narrow understanding of freedom, he can never get what he wants. So, rather than making a direct (external) argument in support of his favored view of freedom and selfhood, Dostoyevsky opted for an indirect (internal) argument that shows how one specific view of the same will collapse of its own devices. This can be an extraordinarily effective type of argument, because it operates with entirely borrowed premises. Granted, it is a 'negative' argument because it shows only that a certain position will fail, leaving open the question of what position might succeed; but its persuasive power lies in its ability to portray a living philosophical view that drives itself into despair.

Now, imagine that in addition to the Underground Man's mode of consciousness, every other philosophical mode of consciousness (drawn from all of human history) was diagnosed and carried to its logical conclusion. And imagine also that all of these modes were lined up starting with the most simple and accessible one, and progressing to the most sophisticated one, which would also by default be the one that is most stable and most satisfying. This is Hegel's project in the *Phenomenology of Spirit*.

Hegel's *Phenomenology* attempts to describe the immanent development of consciousness, from one epistemological, existential, or social mode to the next, until it finally reaches a point where its concepts are fully adequate to its experience. It is an 'immanent' development because consciousness moves from one mode to the next entirely of its own devices, and Hegel's approach is 'phenom-enological' because he tries to describe what is going on from the point of view of consciousness, capturing the fine-grained radically subjective texture of experience. A good phenomenological descrip-tion of experience will resist the importation of concepts and criti-cisms external to the experience described; it is not, then, supposed to be an account of how Hegel wants consciousness to develop, but rather a description of the path that consciousness follows on its own. And just like in Dostoyevsky's novel, what drives the account is the frustration that consciousness experiences when its own concepts seem inadequate to its own experience. Dostoyevsky's Underground Man is a helpful touchstone to remind us that despite Hegel's obscure prose, what he is talking about it not mystical or esoteric; it is just a philosophically rigorous way of looking at an entirely plausible and ordinary notion that emerges from everyday life.

In what follows, I will first (i) explain Hegel's notion of superses-sion, using the first transition in the *Phenomenology*, from 'sense-certainty' to 'perception' as an example, and consider a number of complexities that emerge from this idea, especially his thinking about the irony of going back on a supersession, and then (ii) turn to Hegel's theory of pure and impure recognition. With these basic Hegelian ideas on the table, I can then (iii) follow some of the details and dynamics of the section in the *Phenomenology* titled 'self-alienated spirit,' which considers culture and alienation, a con-cern of Hegel's that carries over from his early writings. Finally, (iv) I will attempt to lay out a condensed version of the entire narrative of the *Phenomenology*, which is intended to be read alongside Hegel's text, including some analysis of the final chapter on 'abso-lute knowledge.'

i. SUPERSESSION AND HEGELIAN IRONY

The *Phenomenology of Spirit* is a kind of *Bildungsroman* (a novel that portrays a character's growth, acculturation, and philosophical development), but one where the protagonist is 'consciousness.' Hegel's main character will initially seem strangely disembodied, but he wants 'consciousness' to have a kind of generality, so as to capture the various types of theories, personalities, and ways of living for both individuals and groups, that are possible today, and that have occurred through history. So, for example, at some points in the *Phenomenology*, it sounds as though 'consciousness' is really a stand-in for a particular philosopher from history, say, Kant or Voltaire; and at other times, 'consciousness' may seem to represent a general theoretical model instead of an identifiable individual. Hegel wants this ambiguity because he thinks that there are general shapes of thought that tend to emerge in a great diversity of contexts. His protagonist will develop through a series of stages or modes, and will acquire new designations on the way: 'consciousness' becomes 'self-consciousness,' and then 'reason.' And at a crucial transition in the book, the protagonist, who had always been conceivable as an individual, becomes a group, a social practice, even an entire culture: the center of the narrative becomes 'spirit' and then 'religion.'

At this point, though, aside from any complexities generated by Hegel's unorthodox protagonist, let us focus for the moment on the transitions from one mode to the next. For Hegel, the kind of transition he is interested in is an *Aufhebung*, usually translated as 'transcendence' or 'sublation'; but the best translation may be 'supersession,' because it avoids a number of misleading connotations associated with the other translations. In the context of the *Phenomenology*, to say that there are supersessions is to say that there are dialectical progressions through which one interpretation of self, knowledge, or life generally, will give way to another, and that the latter interpretation is, in these cases, superior; the latter interpretation is superior because it resolves tensions inherent in the prior stage, or because it better satisfies the criteria established earlier, or because it proves to be a more stable or satisfying interpretation to inhabit and explore than the previous one (PHG §§ 11–59; PH 54–79). In Hegel's view, a supersession is also a 'determinate negation,' in the sense that although one mode of consciousness has been 'negated,' consciousness is nonetheless not stuck in a void but rather able to move in some determinate direction, namely towards a new mode that is potentially more satisfying than the one that has just been negated or superseded (PHG § 59).

As the example of Dostoyevsky's Underground Man suggests, Hegelian supersession is really an intuitively plausible notion, and one that is found in countless examples in everyday life. If Dostoyevsky's case does not seem so ordinary, consider the process through which a child becomes an adult, abandoning views that are naïve, uninformed, or superficial, for new ones that are more sophisticated, informed, satisfying, or deep; any child will undergo a series of supersessions that mirrors in many ways Hegel's account. The difference, though, between this intuitive case of a child's process of maturation and the narrative of the *Phenomenology* is that Hegel is trying to be philosophically rigorous and systematic, an ambition that is probably not shared by most ordinary people. And his starting point, the mode of consciousness that thinks it has immediate knowledge of the world through its senses, might also seem already pretty sophisticated to most people, despite the fact that commentators usually refer to it as 'naïve empiricism.'

In any case, Hegel's initial mode of consciousness is at least philosophically naïve, since it represents a theory of knowledge that passes for common sense among new philosophy students. Hegel calls this mode 'sense-certainty,' and it is characterized by a rather clumsy epistemological orientation: it thinks that its sensory experience of the world is exhaustive, authoritative, and the richest and most immediate source of knowledge of the world (PHG §§ 90–110). This naïve empiricism establishes criteria for knowledge of the world that supposedly can be satisfied exclusively through the senses. But whenever the naïve empiricist attempts to point to an object of which he or she supposedly has knowledge, it turns out to be quite difficult to show convincingly that this is really knowledge. Hegel's argument here is actually an anticipation of what Ludwig Wittgenstein was to argue much later, namely, that it is impossible to state what is simple or complex in any object without consideration of context (and talking about the context would introduce concepts that did not come from sense-experience); naïve empiricism must learn that no 'thing' can ever be pointed out and known without the use of universals that constitute the requisite context (PHG § 97; PI §§ 45–7, 60). For example, if one pointed and said 'that is a broom,' and claimed that the object, the broom, is known immediately, the problem would be that 'that' does not immediately pick anything out. In other words, 'sense-certainty' cannot attain knowledge that fits its own criteria because it cannot say what it has knowledge of and, at the same time, avoid the necessary account of how consciousness utilizes concepts that identify objects as objects, differentiated from the broader manifold of immediate sense-perceptions. 'Sense-certainty,' then, ends up in frustration and collapse, and, according to Hegel, the new mode of consciousness that solves the tensions of 'sense-certainty' is one that acknowledges the role of universals and secondary qualities (PHG §§ 111–31). Hegel calls the new mode 'perception,' and it represents a supersession of 'sense-certainty.'

In Hegel's view, a supersession will count as a kind of cancellation, preservation, and transcendence (ENCI § 96A). The mode of consciousness that has been superseded loses the immediacy and naïve promise that it once held; but since the new mode is a genuine resolution of the tensions of the canceled mode, there is a sense in which the prior mode is preserved, namely in that its mediated form is now part of the awareness of the new mode. Hegel also thinks that although retrogression is always possible, the superseded mode of consciousness could only be taken up ironically (LHP 46). It is impossible, for example, to regain the naïve standpoint of youth, and if one tries nonetheless, it could only be false naiveté, a kind of dissembling; in any case, it would be a mode of consciousness positioned against its own experience in a peculiar, ironic way. In the case of 'sense-certainty,' once one realizes that naïve empiricism can never satisfy the criteria it sets for itself, one is in a position to take up a new way of thinking about knowledge, to take up a new set of criteria the satisfaction of which would constitute knowledge. Hegel argues that an awareness of the role of universals will be distinctive of this new mode and will resolve the tensions of the mode it superseded. And of course, this new mode will have its own tensions and will itself be superseded.

But if this claim, that superseded modes of consciousness can only be taken up ironically, is to be a helpful formulation of Hegel's view, different senses of irony must be distinguished. Consider three kinds of irony: simple, complex, and retrogressive. Simple irony is the common type of irony in contemporary everyday usage, according to which one is ironic when one means the opposite of what one says. For example, after a disastrous performance plagued by technical difficulties, a collective inability to work together, and unforeseen problems with the charts, one musician turns to another and says, 'this gig was a smashing success.' This is a case of simple irony, rather self-contained in a single linguistic expression, where the speaker dissembles by saying the opposite of what she means. The simple ironist does not mean what she says, so her assertions provide a mask, and her interlocutors are left in a position to speculate about what her meaning really is, behind the mask.

In complex irony, though, the speaker both means and does not mean what he or she says. A common interpretation of Socrates takes him to be the paradigmatic example of one who practices complex irony: when he says that he 'does not know anything' or that 'he is not a teacher,' there are two levels of meaning here, because he both means what he says and does not mean what he says. By the ordinary understanding of knowledge and teaching, Socrates means exactly what he says; but with the special philosophical understanding of knowledge and teaching that he defends, he does not mean what he says. Complex irony, then, is a special mode of communication, one in which an esoteric or special meaning is communicated through ordinary language; but in contrast to simple irony, the meaning of what is said is not simply the opposite of the ordinary meaning, but rather the expression of a deeper and more sophisticated understanding of the terms in use alongside their straightforward exoteric meaning. Socrates' case is especially interesting here because he refuses ever to explain that he is employing these two levels of meaning, and so we are left with the interpretive question whether he is really utilizing irony in this complex way, and so also, whether or not he is committed to a particular substantive view that he is in fact teaching to his audience.

Retrogressive irony is similar to simple and complex irony in that it involves a kind of dissembling, the suggestion that there is something more going on than is immediately apparent, but differs in that the retrogressive ironist is not in a position to say or argue about what the larger picture is. Retrogressive irony suggests that something deep has been hidden from view, but without the promise that the depth can be articulated, without the guarantee that anything will ever be unmasked. In the context of modes of consciousness, philosophical views, and ways of life, retrogressive irony merely suggests that battles have been fought and won: one 'goes back' on a supersession by taking up the vocabulary of the superseded view, and implies that one is justified in so doing, that there is a bigger picture that justifies this retrogression. The retrogressive ironist, though, does not know what this bigger picture looks like.

Returning to the example of the naïve empiricist from the *Phenomenology*, it must be pointed out that not all naïve empiricists are equal: the naïve empiricist who has never followed through the phenomenological reflection and experience that Hegel describes is not ironic in any way (he or she is just naïve), but the person who has gone through the supersession and then tries to 'go back' is being retrogressively ironic. This person does not mean the opposite of what he or she says, nor is this person trying to express an esoteric meaning by way of making naïve empiricist claims (though one could imagine a Socratic teacher who uses complex irony to teach something about empiricism). The person who 'goes back' in this fashion implies that we are not getting the whole picture, which would presumably contain an argument that shows the supersession in question to be an illusion; but the smug and self-satisfied retrogressive ironist is not making any attempt to supply this argument. This ironist merely hints and suggests that such an argument is out there, but supplies nothing to substantiate this implication. And again, there is a difference between the sincere naïve empiricist and the retrogressively ironic empiricist: outward appearances and utterances are insufficient without the substantive phenomenological information that would allow one to see the irony in the latter case.

Retrogressive irony is existential, internal, and developmental. It is existential, like complex irony, because it is more than a self-contained speech act: it is a mode of consciousness, a general way of living and relating to others. In the interpretation of Socrates mentioned earlier, his complex irony is clearly more than a mere linguistic trick or trope he occasionally uses; it defines his entire method of teaching and is expressive of his substantive philosophical views. Likewise, the retrogressive ironist is taking up a mode of consciousness akin to those Hegel describes in the *Phenomenology*, namely those defined by general orientations towards knowledge, morality, history, and such; retrogressive irony does not arise outside of those contexts in which it makes sense to speak of supersessions in the first place. Of course, that retrogressive irony is an existential mode of consciousness and not merely a linguistic device is not to rule out the ways that specific claims in language can become ironic when we reflect on them, and this in a way that helps supersessions become clear. For example, in the 'sense-certainty' section of the *Phenomenology*, Hegel points out that the naïve empiricist will realize that he cannot say what he means to say, that language actually refutes what he or she thinks is going on (PHG § 63, 97).

ii. PURE AND IMPURE RECOGNITION

The German word that is typically translated as 'recognition' is *Anerkennung*, and for Hegel it refers to those practical encounters through which one grants to another person a kind of status or standing, namely, as a person and as a moral subject. The sort of status that is granted depends on the context, the sort of normative space in which individuals confront each other. Hegel's account of recognition expresses his view that the freedom that is possible for modern individuals presupposes that self-identity is reinterpreted as inter-subjective self-identity, and that once one has come to acquire this understanding, one can only go back to a narrow assertive self-understanding ironically (retrogressively); through recognition, one comes to see that such a narrow self-identity is impoverished. The recognition story is also an interpretation of what it is to be free, and so it offers both a description of how individuals embrace such an interpretation, and also a sketch of the normative implications of this interpretation. Hegel suggests here that pure recognition is also the foundation of 'spirit,' of the experience of 'the "I" that is "We" and the "We" that is "I",' but at this point in the narrative of the *Phenomenology*, however, consciousness is not ready for this; it only catches a glimpse of 'spirit' before being swept into the dialectic of master and slave (PHG § 177).

Hegel introduces recognition at an important transition in the *Phenomenology*, namely, where he takes himself to have shown how all attempts of consciousness to acquire knowledge of objects as an apprehending, viewing, and observing subject have failed. Despite the various attempts of consciousness to acquire knowledge of things, whether on the model of empiricism or natural science, it becomes clear that the subject can only acquire knowledge of its own concepts, the very concepts that necessarily mediate the things of which it tries to acquire knowledge. With the frustration of the individualist model of acquiring knowledge, Hegel suggests that consciousness will take up a new project, one that is social and practical instead of epistemological. So, consciousness takes up the perspective that it is part of organic life, that it is a living thing with various practical desires. And it is at this point that consciousness is no longer looking for a stable object of knowledge (the general criterion of traditional epistemology according to Hegel), but rather something that is stable and certain inside of itself, something of which it is truly the origin and author.

When consciousness introspects and tries to find something stable and certain, it finds only that it is an organism with many desires, and feels that these desires must be satisfied in the world (PHG §§ 174–6). Hegel suggests that consciousness will only feel independent in a world of external objects, a world of 'others,' if it asserts itself against these objects; the reason this activity generates a sense of independence is that whereas a desire on its own is indeterminate, a desire that is specifically directed against something suggests that there is an agency responsible for the direction and focusing of desire. Consciousness feels empowered and self-determining when it 'negates' external objects; it feels confident of itself when it projects itself into the world in this way, as though it were satisfying its criterion for being free. This sort of 'negating' is to be understood quite literally as a kind of destroying or consuming; the desirous consciousness actively gives its vague desires a shape by directing them through the act of consumption. By consuming the object, as in the case of eating a piece of food, consciousness enjoys the fleeting awareness of self-sufficiency, its own agency against vague desires and foreign objects. But this feeling of empowerment is only temporary, and it soon becomes clear that this primitive mode of consciousness will almost always be in the throws of indeterminate desire, and so will always be looking for another object to consume or destroy; its satisfaction is not permanent.

But what happens if consciousness encounters not an 'object' but another conscious being? This will strike consciousness as a very different situation, and its response will take one of two forms, which will come to represent 'pure recognition' and 'impure recognition' (PHG §§ 178–85; 186–96). The former case represents the ideal inter-subjective interaction, where neither consciousness treats the other as an object to be consumed, but rather confers upon the other the status of free selfhood; the latter case represents the degenerate form, the way recognition often occurs, and was bound to occur historically before there were modern political arrangements to solidify relations of pure recognition.

The first form of Hegel's theory of recognition, pure recognition, consists of three phases or moments: one loses one's abstract atomicity in recognizing the other as like oneself, one tries for self-recovery in soliciting acknowledgment from the other, and both participants recover self-consciousness through mutual recognition (PHG §§ 179–81). In the first phase, consciousness is still in its uncertain desirous state, and is thus engaged in the project of assuring itself of its self-sufficiency by consuming or annihilating objects. But when consciousness encounters another consciousness, the other is perceived as a threat: since the other seems identical, it is not clear that it can be annihilated in the manner of non-identical objects, and thus poses the threat that desirous consciousness may not be able even fleetingly to reassure itself that it is self-directing. Unable to reassure itself of its own agency by shaping its indeterminate desires, the original self-consciousness is lost and set adrift.

The second moment is the attempt to seek acknowledgment from the other that it is in fact an agent with the ability to direct its own actions, and the third moment is the mutual conferral of this status, that is, mutual or pure recognition. In the third moment, each consciousness allows the other to return to its self (since in the first phase they had been 'othered' by seeing themselves in the other). If all three of these phases occur, both individuals get a sense of genuine agency, and the possibility of being truly free. Through mutual recognition, consciousness sees the other as part of itself, not because the other is identical, but because both selves mutually allowed each other to be, each let the other 'go free.' The result of pure recognition is that an individual comes to understand him or herself as a genuinely self-directing agent, not because he or she is radically independent from other objects and persons, but because these are no longer seen as threatening; one is recognized as an individual who can affirm and embrace the paradox that our independence is a kind of dependence.

The other form of Hegel's account of recognition, impure recognition, documents what he thinks happens when mutual recognition fails, where each self-consciousness tries for recognition through the other, but does not initially make any move towards granting recognition to the other. Hegel characterizes this attempt as a 'struggle to the death' because if consciousness attempts to reassure itself in its typical way by treating the other as an object, consciousness must be willing to risk its life in the confrontation. The struggle to the death leads either to the death of one party, which would be self-defeating since there would then not be anyone to grant recognition and allow consciousness to escape the frustrating state of desire, or to the subjugation of one party by the other. In the latter case, the 'dialectic of master and slave' begins and ultimately leads to recognition granted by the 'slave' to the 'master.' This recognition, though, only occurs because the 'slave' loses the battle, or is not willing to risk his or her life; the 'master,' on the other hand, seems to win a significant kind of status, at least initially. Hegel thinks that risking one's life and experiencing the fear of death ('absolute fear') is important because in the face of death, one grapples with the loss of all one's ties to the world and nonetheless takes the goal of attaining the status of free and self-directing individual to be worth it. The willingness to risk life, then, is the willingness to sacrifice these ties, that is, the demonstration that one is not bound by them.

The ironic twist, though, is that the recognition of the 'master' by the 'slave' is not a genuine form of recognition, since the 'master' and the 'slave' are not equals, and even though the 'master' won the struggle to the death, he nonetheless fails to achieve genuine recognition. The 'slave,' though, Hegel suggests, through work and the interaction with the world necessary to satisfy the 'master's' desires, gradually acquires a genuine self-consciousness: the 'slave' moves away from the mode of desire to a form of genuine agency through the work of satisfying an other's desires (PHG §§ 193–6). Indeed, it is the 'slave's' initial decision not to risk life but to maintain ties to the world that re-emerges as a sense of agency and develops into a fully-fledged form.

Hegel's account of pure recognition is intended to be a conceptual argument about what it means to be a genuinely free individual, an individual who is able to identify with his or her actions, choices, and ends, while also acknowledging how these are mediated by others. The argument is critical of the familiar view of freedom and agency based on the self-determination of the radically free will, the view that lurks behind Dostoyevsky's Underground Man. If an individual chases the myth of radical independence and self-determination, he or she will feel that objects, other persons, and even his or her own arbitrary desires are threats to this independence; this person will occupy a perpetually unsatisfying state, a state that offers only the most fleeting satisfaction during the act of consuming objects, or in treating others as objects. Hegel was of course writing about this long before Dostoyevsky wrote his novel, but it is striking how Hegel's account anticipates the turmoil of the Underground Man's experience.

iii. SELF-ALIENATED SPIRIT

The first step in trying to understand any of the sections in the *Phenomenology* is to grasp the initial starting point for the mode of consciousness in question; one must figure out what this mode of consciousness wants, what its assumptions are, and how these translate into specific criteria that it is trying to satisfy. The 'self-alienated spirit' section occurs after the major transition in the book from individual consciousness to social consciousness, and this means that Hegel is looking at consciousness as 'spirit,' as the socially situated forms of consciousness that emerge in history. Prior to the 'self-alienated spirit' section, Hegel has traced the development of 'spirit' from Greek society, which is a stage of 'immediacy' in which individuals recognize themselves as part of the community that establishes the normative order, to Roman society, where consciousness has retreated from the conflicts and confusions of life and withdrawn into itself. In Hegel's view, the transition from Greek to Roman society is triggered by an irreconcilable conflict that emerges in Greek society between 'human' and 'divine' law; this conflict, he says, is expressed in Sophocles' play *Antigone*: the 'divine' law that motivates Antigone to bury her brother Polynices comes into conflict with the 'human' law enforced by Creon that prohibits it. There were two contradictory visions of society that coexisted in Greece, one based on the traditional set of religious and family obligations, and the other based on the emerging rule of law; these two visions could not be reconciled, and ultimately 'spirit' takes up a new vision based on a legalistic conception of individual rights under the law. This new stage is Roman society, which Hegel calls 'legal status.'

The self understanding of 'spirit' in Roman society, Hegel says, is based on its withdrawal from the world and its regrouping under the idea of private property, which is supported by the Roman legal system (PHG § 480). But this creates a new kind of problem, because this sort of legally supported individualism leaves people feeling alienated, atomized, and craving some meaningful connection to the larger community. This is why 'spirit' in Roman society is looking for ways to engage the sphere of culture and generate meaning for individuals that ties them together with a sense of community purpose and shared values. And this section of the *Phenomenology* is important because the tensions that arise in Roman society have re-emerged in modernity; if there are answers to be found for our modern problems, we must understand how these issues first arose in ancient Rome, how they played themselves out, and whether our contemporary situation is different in ways that present new possibilities for us.

The main transformations and stages in the 'self-alienated culture' section are: (i) the move from abstract (pure) determinations of value and judgment to concrete plans of action, (ii) the attempt of the 'feudal lord' to identify with the 'general good,' (iii) the naming of a 'monarch' and the simultaneous shift in power, (iv) the establishment of the Bourgeoisie and the essence of wealth, and finally, (v) the truth of the 'bohemian.' And since the efforts of consciousness in this section ultimately fail, we should understand why this occurs as well.

So, at the beginning of the section on culture, consciousness is removed, isolated, and detached from the world, now forced to view the world as an alien, external, and unyielding thing, since nothing in the self-conception of consciousness includes the elements of the culture in which it finds itself (PHG § 484). Consciousness is now aware of two possible modes: the first is the one it currently inhabits, which is removed from the world, and the second, which remains at this point only a possibility, is one which lies in the world, engaged with it and embodying all of its movement and turmoil (PHG § 485). But even though this mode of consciousness occupies the first form, and knows that it is responsible for this, it still views the world as its true essence (PHG §§ 489–90). This is a problem because consciousness sees its own essence outside of itself, and in hostile confrontation. The strategy consciousness chooses as a remedy, and this strategy is the main theme of the section, is one which involves the sacrifice of its individuality, its atomicity and legal status, so as to take on the content of society and the world. Without such a sacrifice, one cannot hope to acquire any kind of universality, and will remain stuck, as it were, in the position of an isolated atom (PHG § 484).

This is of course a general theme in Hegel's *Phenomenology*, and it can be described in various ways: as the need to create one's essence through self-sacrifice or renunciation, the strategy of overcoming alienation (*Entfremdung*) through alienation (*Entäusse-*

rung), or, more poetically, how one must 'lose oneself to find oneself' (PHG § 18). For Hegel, what is needed is a renunciation that is a real sacrifice, the adoption of a new sort of selfhood that 'negates' the aspirations of the original self (PHG § 503). The original self that consciousness has latched onto is the atomized self that is related to the social whole only negatively, as that which is not the whole. This atomized individual is defined in terms of individual rights of property, that is, boundaries that separate that individual from the larger society; holding fast to one's 'personhood' here precludes one's ability to recognize oneself in anything larger than narrowly defined individual pursuits. For this individual to engage in sacrifice and self-renunciation, he or she must act against these boundaries and against this kind of self-interest.

Hegel adds that if consciousness engages in sacrifice and renunciation, it will have a 'double effect': sacrificing for the sake of a universal and common good will automatically make that good more 'real' for the simple reason that someone is acting for it and recognizing it. The individual sacrifices and actions are, as Hegel would put it, 'manifestations of that universal' (PHG § 490). It is a double effect because that to which one sacrifices is created and strengthened through that very act: one creates the very social reality which becomes the content of the newly emerging self. This dual aspect of sacrifice and renunciation on the one hand, and appropriation and creation on the other, provides a fuller meaning, of Hegel's claim that consciousness 'takes possession' of the world that it confronts (PHG § 488, 490).

Returning to the developmental story at hand, consciousness is withdrawn and removed from the world, but finds itself confronted with a social setting complete with the rudimentary forms of power structures and institutions, and it wants to engage it in the right way. So, it first applies to the cultural world it confronts the basic intuitive distinction between 'good' and 'bad' (PHG § 491). Since the two main power-generating institutions in post-Roman society are the state and private wealth, 'good' is identified with the state, as that which is 'universal,' and 'bad' is identified with personal wealth, since it lacks any 'universal' or general value (PHG § 494). But since consciousness has not yet committed to any particular engagement with the world, it still contemplates its choices in a non-committal fashion (PHG §§ 494–5). With some reflection, though, consciousness realizes that there are equally forceful arguments for reversing its initial designations of 'good' and 'bad,' since the state could be oppressive, and personal wealth could be a shield against this oppression. Consciousness concludes that no abstract analysis of what is 'good' and what is 'bad' will be helpful here, so it will need a new way of considering its options (PHG §§ 495–8).

Consciousness then tries the alternative distinction between 'likeness' and 'disparity,' with their correlated terms, 'noble' and 'ignoble,' in the hopes that this will suggest a viable way to engage the sphere of culture and overcome alienation (PHG § 499). The noble consciousness identifies either the state or wealth as its essence, and the ignoble consciousness sees only disparity and views the state and wealth with contempt (PHG §§ 500–01). The sense in which the noble consciousness can enter into a 'likeness' relation with wealth and yet not take on a self-interested course of action stems from the fact that wealth, in theory at least, can be enjoyed by anyone, and is not intrinsically good or bad (PHG § 494). Consciousness concludes that it should strive to become noble, because this promises a unity with some form of universality or other; whereas the ignoble course should be avoided, because it cannot identify with anything and will naturally become hostile towards any such institution (PHG § 501).

At this point, the main theme of the section, the idea of self-sacrifice for the sake of self-transcendence, finally takes a concrete form, and the idea that each mode of consciousness has its own account of what it is trying to accomplish becomes clear (PHG § 502). It is also from this point on that Hegel roughly correlates the stages of development here with the historical periods of feudalism, absolutism, and bourgeois society. This, then, completes the first stage of the section: the move from abstract determinations and judgments to concrete plans of action.

The next stage involves the feudal lord's identification with and sacrifice for the state. This identification finds the lord placing all of his self-directed interests behind the interests of the state, even to the extent of sacrificing his life for the state in battle (PHG

§§ 506–7). This is an example of the 'double effect' of self-sacrifice: the lord's service is recognized by others, and that service makes the state more powerful, which then recursively makes the service seem more meaningful and 'universal' (PHG §§ 504–5). But this only works if the state convincingly represents the 'general good'; it turns out, though, that because there are many lords making sacrifices, each with their own motivations and interests, any 'general good' is undetermined and elusive. This in turn leaves the lord to wonder whether he is still acting from narrow self-interest (PHG § 506).

When a single monarch emerges to consolidate the various interpretations of the common good, the noble consciousness once again attempts to identify with this new universality as a meaningful form of self-sacrifice (PHG § 511). But everyone sees that this is arbitrary and fragile: the lords realize that the monarch's power depends on their recognition, and the monarch realizes this as well, and accordingly distributes wealth to the lords, to preserve and harmonize the new power structure (PHG § 512). The nobles preserve the status of the monarch through the language of flattery, but since they are at the same time receiving wealth, it is an obvious pretense (PHG § 513). So, the current stage of development is this: the nobles named and recognized a single will, a monarch, in an effort to consolidate their differing views of the general good, but in so doing, their power of recognition passed over the monarch and returned to them in the form of wealth. The nobles now stand in an immediate relationship to wealth, and so cultivate their relationship to wealth while at the same time retaining their superficial identification to the quasi-universal will, that is, the monarch (PHG §§ 514–15). Actual power, in the form of wealth, has therefore landed back in the hand of the nobles thus initiating their slide to base consciousness (PHG § 513).

In the fourth stage of the section, Hegel argues that the noble consciousness has fully degenerated into the base consciousness, and now identifies directly with wealth (PHG §§ 514–16). Consciousness now sees its own identity dissolve away, since it can no longer identify what is essential and what is non-essential, and since it now has even less to identify with then at the beginning of the section:

whereas before it at least had a viable, albeit narrow and isolated, conception of the self as a legally defined 'person,' now consciousness can only latch on to wealth (PHG §§ 517–18). This establishment of Bourgeois society, the degeneration of noble consciousness to base consciousness, is therefore at once its demise (PHG § 513). The poor individual in Bourgeois society, knowing that wealth is what defines individuals, sees his or her 'self' dependent upon and displayed by those other individuals who possess wealth; likewise, the rich individual in Bourgeois society wallows in arrogance, feeling that he or she acquires the 'I' of others through wealth and forces them into submission (PHG § 517, 519).

It is from this degeneration and disintegration that we arrive at the fifth and final stage of the section, the emergence of the 'bohemian,' who speaks the 'truth' of the entire progression (PHG § 520). The 'bohemian' most likely emerges from the poor, since he or she is rejecting the debasement of their identity rather than being blinded to it by arrogance, and it is this person who sees and knows that none of the distinctions hitherto mentioned, 'good,' 'bad,' 'noble,' or 'base,' have any meaning (PHG § 517, 521). All of these values and determinations have become inverted and useless (PHG §§ 521–3). The language of the 'bohemian' is the perfect truth of this section, since it is full of contradiction and absurdity; this will seem humorous to like-minded folks, but frustrating and annoying to anyone who clings to the established normative system of bourgeois society (PHG § 521, 524). The 'bohemian' shows why all of the efforts of self-sacrifice have failed: none of the objects of sacrifice remain fixed, their meaning is constantly shifting. At this point in history, the contradictions of wealth, power, and authority undermine any attempts to make sense of the normative structure of society (PHG §§ 523–4). Consciousness concludes that it cannot find meaning in social roles, because there is simply too much contingency and contradiction at play for any meaning to be stable. So consciousness turns to 'faith,' on the reasoning that if meaning is not working out in this world, perhaps it fares better in the otherworldly; and so, off to the next mode goes consciousness.

This section of the *Phenomenology*, then, lays out a structural explanation of why people's efforts to identify with the whole will fail. It is quite possible for people to misunderstand the sort of self-sacrifice Hegel considers, and this would prevent them from finding a satisfying match between self- and social-identity. But the difficulty that is more characteristic of modern culture is, what we might call, 'structural disorientation': the failure to render a coherent and satisfying account of what is 'right' and 'wrong,' and 'good' and 'bad,' in one's culture. One's normative concepts are often too abstract and simplistic to apply to our complex society with any stability. Hegel also thinks that structural disorientation can result from an attempt to move directly from an egoistic perspective to a universal one where there is no intermediate sphere of interaction in which consciousness can be educated and developed. Hegel sees this failure as being located historically, prior to the development of the modern state.

The solution to this kind of disorientation, and the self-defeating efforts that result, is twofold. First, there has to be some real determinacy with what the general good actually is; there cannot be such a multiplicity of goods that no one is able to fashion a strategy of identification (PHG §§ 505–6). Second, there must be mediating institutions that provide a bridge from the narrow individualism of civil society to the general good that is advocated by the state. The 'world of culture' that Hegel diagnoses in the *Phenomenology* is a kind of inchoate version of civil society, but in this undeveloped form of civil society, there is no state that it is distinguished from, and it does not contain the legal institutions or voluntary associations found in modern civil society. It is not sufficient, then, for the elimination of *Entfremdung* that one engages in any kind of *Entäusserung*, though it might be said that this is indeed a necessary condition. It must also be the case, that the institutional structures one identifies with through *Entäusserung* are expressive of a determinate conception of the general good, organized into a coherent state, and that there exist mediating structures to fill the gap between egoism and universalism. Without these conditions satisfied, Hegel argues, an individual's attempt to orient him- or herself in normative space will fail. This analysis, then, points directly to the need for a state that embraces a politics of the common good.

iv. THE PATH TO ABSOLUTE KNOWLEDGE

The *Phenomenology of Spirit* has five main sections ('consciousness,' 'self-consciousness,' 'reason,' 'spirit,' and 'religion'), and then a final chapter on 'absolute knowledge.' There is a dramatic and qualitative break between 'reason' and 'spirit,' which consists in the move from individual consciousness to social or collective consciousness ('spirit'). This transition to 'spirit' is the most difficult move for consciousness to make, and it serves to remind us that although Hegel thinks there is some necessity to this move from the point of view of the philosopher looking backwards and reconstructing the narrative, there is no necessity when it comes to actual manifestations of consciousness, that is, real persons. Moving from 'reason' to 'spirit' is a qualitative leap that can be resisted: empirical consciousness may hang on to its atomized perspective and never move on. But regardless, the philosophical narrative continues towards 'absolute knowledge,' which retains the essential features of that all-important move from individual to social knowing.

The first main section, 'consciousness,' begins with the most natural and naïve mode of consciousness, which attempts to acquire knowledge of immediate objects in the world. This mode of consciousness presupposes a fixed distinction between subject and object, and seeks to satisfy the criterion of a stable, unmediated object. Consciousness struggles with the failure of naïve empiricism ('sense-certainty') to acquire knowledge directly from the senses, and with 'perception's' unfruitful attempt to solve the conceptual difficulties that emerge when one backs away from the senses. The 'understanding' takes up a view akin to modern natural science, positing forces and laws, but ultimately cannot find a stable object of knowledge, and ends up confronting an utterly ungraspable world (the 'inverted world').

The truth of this first section is that there is no stable, fixed, unmediated object of knowledge to be found, but the last effort of consciousness to resist this conclusion at least stumbles across the fruitful concept of 'infinity': consciousness wonders whether all of its distinctions so far (between 'one' and 'many,' 'universal' and 'particular,' and 'thing' and 'its opposite') are contained harmoniously within the world considered as a 'unity' (PHG §§ 160–1). But consciousness is still trying to grasp this 'infinity' or 'unity' as an 'object' of knowledge that can be known by a 'subject' and it fails in its attempt to do this. But the phenomenologist, the occasional narrator of the *Phenomenology*, understands that consciousness has in fact stumbled across something that it is not ready to grasp: 'infinity' not as 'object,' but as the 'unity of subject and object,' which is a glimpse of 'absolute knowledge (PHG §§ 164–5). Consciousness (now in the form of what Hegel calls 'the understanding') tries to describe this 'infinity' as an 'object' and, ostensibly failing once again to make it stable, begins to describe self-consciousness (PHG § 163).

The starting point of 'self-consciousness' is generated from the exhaustion of the attempt to find a stable object and the nascent realization of naïve consciousness that in losing all determination of the 'other,' it has become able to affirm its 'self' (PHG § 167). Consciousness now attempts to grasp the 'infinity' of organic things, that is, 'life' (PHG § 168). Like the 'infinity' of the previous section, 'life' dissolves difference and distinction, and is a flowing, always splitting-up, always regrouping, living things (PHG §§ 171–2). But like naïve consciousness before it, the newly formed self-consciousness is not ready for fully grasping 'life'; rather, it feels threatened by the fleeting appearances of the world, and needs to convince itself that these appearances are really just manifestations of itself. Consciousness tries to negate this threat by consuming it, but when another consciousness shows up and cannot be so easily consumed, the dialectic of 'master' and 'slave' begins.

'Self-consciousness' wants to establish and confirm a stable and independent sense of selfhood, but reacting to the 'master' and 'slave' dialectic, it withdraws into 'skepticism' and then 'stoicism.' 'Self-consciousness' then postulates an unchangeable self, in the hopes that this otherworldly ideal will be helpful, but this only leads to the 'unhappy consciousness,' where one becomes increasingly away of one's feeble imperfections and limitations, to the point of losing all sense of self. The transition into 'reason,' the third main section of the book, follows from self-consciousness' realization that through the power of reason it can overcome the misery of its subordinate relationship to the 'unchangeable' (PHG §§ 227–8, 230). In 'reason,' though, the criterion is the same as in 'self-consciousness,' namely, to assert the stability and independence of selfhood. 'Reason' first attempts to discover rationality, that is, its own 'self,' in nature, through observation, and ultimately ends up in the absurd position of finding itself in a 'dead thing' (PHG §§ 344–5). 'Reason' then turns to itself and its own activity in yet another attempt to satisfy the criterion, but, whether the self-consciousness of 'reason' tries to do this through the pursuit of pleasure, the imposition of virtue on the world, narcissistic self-expression, or the production and testing of moral laws, the result in each case is again failure.

The transition to 'spirit' marks an abrupt change from the strivings of individual modes of consciousness to social modes, which immediately shifts the terms of argument from talk of the abstract individualities, removed from any real context, to talk of 'spirit' as something that signifies the thoughts and activities of real groups of human individuals (PHG § 440). 'Spirit' now takes on the meaning real, human, historical consciousness and includes the content of concrete social and political contexts (PHG § 441). And with 'spirit' there is a twofold movement: as consciousness identifies more with its object, thereby breaking down the distinction between subject and object, and thus becoming more universal, 'social substance' is also actualized to a greater extent with individual consciousness as its manifestation. It is only when the entire community of individuals participates that 'spirit,' the actualization of this unity, for the first time becomes real.

The transition from 'reason' to 'spirit' is also a transition from a position where consciousness has not been able to grasp the richness of 'infinity' (and 'life') to a position where this is seriously grasped for the first time. Hegel's view is that this is only a possibility for social consciousness and not individual consciousness. Earlier, at the transition from 'consciousness' to 'self-consciousness,' Hegel says that what still lies ahead is the experience of 'spirit,' that is, not just the fleeting confrontation with it, but the act of recognizing oneself in it. One has to see 'infinity' (and 'life') as a reflection of oneself, and given that it ultimately includes all other people, the state, religion, etc., the point at which consciousness can begin to know 'the "I" that is "We" and "We" that is "I",' is with the introduction of collective consciousness (PHG § 177). This is why the second part of the *Phenomenology*, where consciousness (now self-consciousness) confronts the actual social world and identifies with it, is necessary.

The progression from Greek society to the French Revolution is the preliminary effort of consciousness (now 'spirit') to see itself in its other, which is the social world; but the progression ends in failure (PHG § 677). Since this initial movement ends in the French Revolution's return to individuality and atomization, 'spirit' must make another attempt to see itself in its other. The historical forms of 'spirit' after the French Revolution are retrogressive: consciousness withdraws into itself, away from the social world, and falls into a paralyzing inability to judge or forgive. The transition to 'religion,' not entirely dissimilar to the transition into 'spirit,' is a move to the community, the social group, as that which can overcome the contradictions of the individual perspective.

The movement in 'religion' is the self-consciousness of 'spirit' attempting to become the object of its own consciousness (PHG § 678). 'Natural religion' and 'religion in the form of art' progressively come closer to a conceptual understanding of the unity of subject and object, and away from 'picture-thinking,' but these modes of consciousness cannot progress far enough. In the section just prior to 'absolute knowledge,' 'revealed religion,' Hegel attempts to describe the relationship between religious consciousness and the figure of Christ. In Christianity, the 'revealed religion,' the unity of the particular and the universal is literally revealed in the form of a human person, a human self-consciousness. Hegel explains that, in this case, the believer does not join the thought of the universal (God) with the particular (existence) in his or her head; rather, the believer sees, hears, and feels an actual person's presence and sees God in that person (PHG § 758). The Christian believer sees in the figure of Christ not any abstract idea of 'goodness' or 'the holy,' but rather the self-consciousness of God: it is the unity of the divine and the human (PHG § 759). Hegel remarks that it is in this union that the divine achieves its highest essence: what 'revealed religion' comes to know is the self that is simultaneously universal and particular (PHG §§ 760–1). But the relationship of consciousness to this content is just a kind of 'picture-thinking': the unity of universal and particular does not include consciousness. Rather, the unity is only seen as an 'other,' from which consciousness remains alienated. The unity that the consciousness of 'revealed religion' reflects upon is, according to Hegel, the content of truth, but it is only grasped in a mystified form (PHG §§ 794–5). It is the demystification of this unity which brings us to 'absolute knowledge,' to 'science,' where the unity of universal and particular is seen as part of the 'I' (PHG §§ 798–9).

'Absolute knowledge' is the final mode of consciousness in the progression of the *Phenomenology*. This final stage is the result of consciousness' despair, frustration, and exhaustion, experienced through all the stages on the way (PHG § 20). In the main body of this chapter, that is, those paragraphs which describe and explain 'absolute knowledge' as a discrete stage in the development of consciousness, Hegel attempts to say what exactly this kind of knowing is, and how it relates to all the previous sections of the book (PHG §§ 798–804). As he recapitulates the overall narrative of the book, he emphasizes two transformations in particular: (i) the move from 'reason' to 'spirit,' where the necessity of social knowing and social selfhood is established, and (ii) the move in 'revealed religion' from 'picture-thinking' to the first grasping of the unity of particular and universal.

One possible explanation of how each of the five main sections link up to 'absolute knowledge' is suggested by Hegel earlier in the book: he uses a metaphor of a 'line broken at the nodes' from which many lines extend towards 'absolute knowledge,' and goes on to say that each of these lines are manifestations of 'spirit' (PHG § 681). Putting the 'truth' of each section alongside each other, with this idea in mind, can only yield the very general notion that each section evidences a movement towards 'infinity,' or the dissolving of the distinction between subject and object. Since each section is an 'attribute' from the perspective of 'spirit,' it is perhaps best to say that each section is an attribute of 'absolute knowledge' insofar as each section is a part of the exposition of the entire progression.

Hegel says in the Preface that his view, his system, can only be justified in its exposition, as a whole with all of its parts, and the central thing we find in this exposition is the gradual expression of the unity of subject and object (PHG §§ 17, 19–20).

In speaking of the move to 'science,' Hegel is commenting on the status of the meta-narrative that has pulled together the various movements throughout the *Phenomenology*. For the individual who possesses 'absolute knowledge,' the meta-narrative must disappear because 'self-consciousness' must recognize itself in all of its externalizations. Attaining 'absolute knowledge' is tantamount to becoming a phenomenologist (PHG §§ 87–9). In 'absolute knowledge,' the distinction between subject and object dissolves, not one into the other, but rather, the distinction itself dissolves as subject and object enter into a kind of harmony. Any object or form of consciousness which might otherwise be understood as 'alien' or 'other' is in fact comprehended and recognized as part of the self of consciousness, and consciousness is fully aware of this unified recognition (PHG §§ 17–18, 89).

There has been a recurring dynamic sequence in each section of the book, from 'immediacy' to 'mediation' to 'essence,' but it would be a mistake to think that this was the formal core of 'absolute knowledge.' Hegel argues that such an abstract schema would lead to a 'boring show of diversity,' or a 'monochromatic formalism' (PHG § 15). It is rather, he says, just the shape of the coming-to-be of 'absolute knowledge,' and applies only to the development of naïve consciousness (PHG § 789). This is not to say that the movement from immediacy to essence is unimportant for grasping that which leads to a particular determinate negation, or the general movement of negation and preservation, just that we should not expect to find 'absolute knowledge' in this form (PHG § 79, 113). Just saying that 'absolute knowledge' is the unity of subject and object, though, is not immediately informative and does not express all that should be contained within it (PHG § 20); even talking about the 'unity of subject and object' as if the components of this unity preserved their original meaning is misleading (PHG § 39). It is also not the case, as implied by the previous statement, that this unity is anything like 'seeing' and 'understanding' both subject and object and alternating between them; that would be nothing more than 'whirling circle' of perception (PHG § 131).

In the text of the chapter on 'absolute knowledge,' Hegel mentions three aspects of this form of knowledge which are important: reality, time, and history. The 'reality' of 'absolute knowledge' can only occur if 'spirit,' the unity of subject and object, knows itself as 'spirit,' that is, there has to be an 'absolute knower.' 'Absolute knowledge' is first present, but not fully 'real,' in self-consciousness as abstract moments, and it gradually becomes more real as self-consciousness includes all its objects in itself (PHG § 801). The issue of time concerns the development of consciousness: the whole is prior to the moments of its discovery, and it remains stuck in time until all of its moments are discovered. There is no other possible way to acquire 'absolute knowledge' than by going through the painful steps of consciousness one step at a time, in time: truth is not a minted coin ready-made (PHG § 39). No one could skip to the final pages and understand anything of what Hegel is trying to say. The main parts of the progression of consciousness become timeless upon completion of the 'system,' which, in Hegel's case, could only occur upon attaining 'absolute knowledge' (PHG § 679). Finally, with the idea of history, Hegel means to emphasize the actual labors and despair of the modes of consciousness that are manifest in the stages of history.

One basic theme of 'absolute knowledge,' and of Hegel's philosophy generally, which ties the above mentioned characteristics to the activity of 'absolute knowing,' is the idea of sacrifice and surrender. And this reinforces the idea that 'absolute knowledge' is an activity; it would seem inconsistent if, after discussing each mode of consciousness through the entire *Phenomenology* as ways of living, Hegel would arrive at 'absolute knowledge' and consider it only as a theory or collection of interesting ideas. Further, exercising the knowledge of the unity of the subject and the object is much more than just applying a set of formal concepts to the object and experience; it is not, as Hegel puts it, 'a lifeless schema' which is used to simply multiply the various determinations of the object (PHG § 50). It is rather the case that for understanding to be 'scientific,' it must surrender itself to the object, it must lose itself in its object

(PHG § 53). Hegel speaks of avoiding the ready-made and abstract tools of shallow philosophy and instead really 'tarrying' with negative and the difficult; to become preoccupied with acquiring knowledge, one must surrender to the issue in question (PHG §§ 3, 32–3). Likewise, each stage in the development of consciousness should be lingered over, with all of its pain and despair (PHG § 29). Only then will one 'lose oneself' in the object, and only then will one enjoy the effects of the 'double movement': this only occurs when each side, subject and object, posits the other and creates the unified whole by dissolving themselves in it (PHG § 42, 61). It should be remembered as well that, just prior to the attainment of 'absolute knowledge,' it is not just the subject that is partial in its viewing the object as separate and alien, but also substance itself (PHG § 37). When this defect is overcome, when there is no separation between truth and knowledge, the *Phenomenology of Spirit* is concluded.

In other words, 'absolute knowledge' is a way of losing oneself in a problem, without clinging either to the 'object' or to one's 'self' in the vain hope of explaining the problem away. One must seek out contradictions and 'tarry with the negative' (PHG § 804). The *Phenomenology* is about the actual shapes of consciousness on the way to 'absolute knowledge,' but upon its completion, where the truths of the main sections become attributes, and when consciousness steps out of time grasps 'infinity' and 'life,' there must be a system of concepts which articulates this unity; Hegel will need to complete his 'system' so that the 'absolute knower' can use these concepts (PHG § 805). Hegel says that at this point that we have returned to 'sense-certainty,' which means that we have returned to the immediate relationship with what seems to be the 'richest and fullest' knowledge, but whereas 'sense-certainty' was an illusion, now it is true (PHG § 806). And finally, it is of course also the task of the 'absolute knower' to recollect the progression of the *Phenomenology*, since this remains the 'science' of what was necessary for 'absolute knowledge' (PHG § 808).

As a final note, and to restate the main idea: 'infinity' (and 'life') plays a central role in the *Phenomenology* because it must be grasped by consciousness if that consciousness is to grasp 'absolute knowledge,' and no consciousness can do that alone. The abandonment of the individual mode of consciousness is the most important and difficult step that consciousness must take. 'Absolute knowledge' is not an individual possession, and any philosopher who lives isolated in the dusty corners of the library, no matter how many books are consumed there, will never escape despair.

CHAPTER 4

HEGEL'S *ENCYCLOPEDIA*: THE STRUCTURE OF BEING, NATURE, AND MIND

Each of the parts of philosophy is a philosophical whole, a circle that closes upon itself; but in each of them the philosophical Idea is in a particular determinacy or element. Every single circle also breaks through the restrictions of its element as well, precisely because it is inwardly [the] totality, and it grounds a further sphere. The whole presents itself therefore as a circle of circles, each of which is a necessary moment, so that the system of its peculiar elements constitutes the whole Idea – which equally appears in each single one of them. (ENCI § 15)

Contemporary research in evolutionary biology has documented a number of cases of convergent evolution, where unrelated organisms (or at least very distantly related organisms) acquire similar traits over time as they adapt to similar environments: fish living in the cold waters around the earth's poles have independently developed anti-freeze proteins in their blood; tuna and Mako sharks have independently developed a muscular structure that allows them to swim faster; isolated populations of stickleback fish have evolved in almost identical ways since the last ice age; and the mechanics of vision and the eye have been independently reinvented by organisms repeatedly through natural history. And there are also basic structural features shared by many different organisms that suggest convergence, for example, the basic wing structure of bats, birds, and pterodactyls, and also the general 'anteater' design that we find expressed by animals in Australia, Africa, and America.

Philosophers who are currently writing about evolution (for example, Daniel Dennett) have become interested in cases of convergent evolution because they reveal the existence of 'forced moves' in nature (DDI 128). The idea of a 'forced move' comes from chess, where there is often a board position that forces a particular move, lest one inevitably and immediately (or almost immediately) lose the game. Forced moves in this context are not required by the rules of chess, nor are they required by the laws of physics; it is rather just that such moves are necessary in light of the goal of winning. In the context of evolutionary biology, a forced move is an adaptation that an organism must acquire lest it die out, and in certain local conditions, such adaptations will seem to us like rather obvious solutions to specific engineering problems in the design space of nature.

Evolutionary biologists must be careful about distinguishing between convergent evolution and homology (similar characteristics due to shared ancestry, as in the case of mammalian ear bones and reptilian jaw bones) or other forms of contingency that appear as necessity (for example, 'qwerty' phenomenon, referring to the sequence of keys across the top row of a modern typewriter: it could have been a different sequence originally, but now the sequence is deeply entrenched and reliably passed on). There will always be complexities in sorting out which forms of necessity are mathematical, logical, or physical, and which can ultimately be traced back to contingent historical conditions that could be this way or that, and that sometimes foreclose design options in the future. But careful study of convergent evolution allows us to assemble an account of nature that teases necessity away from contingency by identifying the basic organizing principles of nature, and thereby revealing its *a priori* structure. And once we are doing this, we are squarely engaged in exactly what Hegel took himself to be doing in his philosophy of nature, namely, trying to reconstruct the basic organizing principles of nature, which are only incompletely revealed in observable events.

Of course, the philosophy of nature is just one part of the system that Hegel develops in his *Encyclopedia of the Philosophical Sciences* (first published in 1817, followed by revised editions in 1827 and 1830). The 'system' as a whole reconstructs the basic organizing principles and structure of what exists, first at the level of concepts and thought itself (part one, the *Encyclopedia Logic*, which is the condensed version of the *Science of Logic*), then in terms of how this structure is manifest in nature (part two, the *Philosophy of Nature*), and finally in light of the emergence of 'spirit,' with special attention to how humanity has come to reflect on its deepest values and interests, which are mediated by the structure of both thought and nature, and the necessity that humanity's collective reflection occur in the context of particular states, institutions, and cultural practices (part three, the *Philosophy of Mind*). This chapter begins with an example from biology, which might suggest an awkward entry into the middle of the 'system,' but the philosophy of nature offers an accessible foothold for Hegel's contemporary readers; the overall project of the *Encyclopedia* is obscure enough to most readers without also requiring that they comprehend the *Logic* just as they begin venturing into the 'system.'

When starting straightaway with the *Logic*, the first challenge to getting one's bearings is that Hegel's metaphysical commitments are not at all clear. His view defies easy classification here, because although he is surely committed to a metaphysics of some sort, it is not the familiar and historically entrenched metaphysics of substance, but rather what we might call a 'metaphysics of structure.' So one challenge of the *Logic* is that it forces us to reconsider what a 'metaphysics' is, which requires us to adopt a new vocabulary for addressing the issue; another challenge is the subject matter of the *Logic* itself, which Hegel tells us is the structure of thought itself, apart from any particular consciousness engaged in the thinking of thought.

The distinction between a 'metaphysics of structure' and a metaphysics of substance, then, is much easier to grasp in the context of nature, because the task of looking for the basic structure and organizing principles of nature is a familiar one, given the centrality of scientific inquiry in our modern culture. The *Philosophy of Nature* is still a challenge to our typical metaphysical assumptions, but it nonetheless tends to avoid the sort of paralyzing disorientation often produced by the *Logic*. The convergent evolution case puts Hegel's philosophy in dialogue with the questions and findings of contemporary evolutionary biology, and shows at least that Hegel's view is no more fanciful than what we take to be legitimate science by today's standards.

It is also helpful to consider evolutionary theory in particular, because Hegel notably rejected the evolutionary theory of his day. Granted, he was writing over thirty years before the publication of Darwin's *Origin of Species*, but all the same, Hegel goes out of his way to reject the evolutionary arguments that were then being debated; revisiting the reasons why he thought he needed to reject evolution will clarify his view of the structure of nature, as well as the entire project of the *Encyclopedia*. The perhaps surprising result of this is that we must now interpret Hegel's philosophy as fully consonant with the basic claims of evolutionary theory, which in any case makes his view much more plausible and interesting than it has seemed to so many commentators in recent generations.

The third part of the *Encyclopedia*, the *Philosophy of Mind*, concerns the emergence of 'spirit' from nature, the development of 'spirit' into modern political institutions and the state, and introduces the terminology of 'subjective,' 'objective,' and 'absolute' spirit. It is here that Hegel starts to develop his view of the modern state and political life that will appear in full form in the *Philosophy of Right*.

In this chapter, I will be concerned mainly with material in the *Encyclopedia* up to and including the emergence of 'spirit' from nature; this leaves out most of the *Philosophy of Mind*, but since that part of the *Encyclopedia* is greatly expanded in the *Philosophy of Right*, I will leave the issues it treats for the next chapter. The main issues and arguments under consideration here are: (i) the ambiguous relationship between the *Phenomenology* and the 'system,' (ii) the role of the 'understanding' and 'reason' in the *Logic*, (iii) teleology, evolution, and the philosophy of nature, and (iv) the emergence of 'spirit.'

i. THROWING AWAY THE LADDER

Although Hegel spent most of his career arguing that the *Phenomenology of Spirit* was the proper introduction to his system, and although this has largely been taken as the 'official' position on the matter, its relation to the rest of his works is ambiguous. Many commentators have pointed out that most of the substance of the *Phenomenology* appears in the third book of the *Encyclopedia*, and also in expanded form in a number of Hegel's other major works; this suggests that the former might best be interpreted as a first draft of the 'system' that was simply reworked and expanded. But Hegel exacerbated this ambiguity when, at the end of his career, he seemed to have changed his mind and starting thinking that nothing was needed beyond the text of the *Encyclopedia* itself. There is no consensus among scholars about how to handle this ambiguity, but for our purposes, nothing hangs on it: just raising the question, and considering some of the connections and contrasts between these two books will go a long way towards making clear what Hegel's 'system' is about.

If we accept the view that the *Phenomenology* is the necessary introduction to the system, it would be natural to assume that there must be some set of substantive claims or realizations that is carried over into the beginning of the *Logic*. Recall from the previous chapter that the most important feature of 'absolute knowledge' is the realization that the individual modes of knowing and individual modes of trying to be free are limited; these individualized modes of consciousness cannot get what they want, and must be supplanted by social modes of knowing and social modes of becoming free. Knowing and becoming free must be social or 'minded' (*geistlich*) projects if they are to be philosophically satisfying. And closely connected with this realization is the corollary notion that knowledge and freedom are mediated by history, and that 'absolute knowledge' is an historical achievement. And we might add to this some realization of the unity of subject and object, which occurs as consciousness finally 'loses itself' in its object, as well as some comprehension of the need for a system of concepts to elaborate this unity, lest it all become a quasi-mystical and blank reference.

Only after internalizing the conclusions of the *Phenomenology*, then, are we in a position to reconstruct the structure of thought itself, and to engage in what Hegel considers genuine philosophical thinking. But still, we should not imagine that thinking about thinking will come naturally, or will yield concepts which are 'familiar' (ENCI §§ 2–3, 19, 20). The activity of making thought into an object for itself, Hegel says, comes out of meditative thinking (*nachdenken*) and expresses the dialectic as its essential nature (ENCI § 11). And the dialectic will unfold in the form of a system, a 'circle of circles' that contains all previous philosophical principles (ENCI §§ 13–15). What we will find through this process, Hegel adds, is that the whole interrelated system of categories or concepts will be 'brought to light,' which means that we will find the structures that have already been operating in our thinking; when we see this, we will be 'at home with ourselves' and 'free' in our thinking activity (ENCI §§ 19, 23–4, 27, 31). Indeed, what we unveil is our essential nature as humans, that is, that it is our thinking that separates us from other animals, and this thinking determines what we are (ENCI §§ 20–1). But again, it is not the 'I' who becomes free here, in the manner of the struggling consciousness of the *Phenomenology*; it is rather, as Hegel puts it, the 'struggle of reason' (ENCI § 23, 32). Hegel explains that in the *Logic*, we are supposed to proceed 'descriptively and argumentatively,' which seems to suggest that we should be carrying out all inferences that are warranted given certain concepts, and that these inferences will be the motor behind the elaboration of the whole system of concepts.

The first category of the *Logic* is supposed to be the most abstract, indeterminate, pure, and immediate thought possible, namely, 'being.' This concept of 'being' is so indeterminate that 'nothingness' cannot even be distinguished from it, so there is a kind of instability between them. If we think about it 'descriptively and argumentatively,' we find that we cannot make a claim about 'being' that is not also a claim about 'nothingness.' Once we see that any claim we try to make will necessarily recruit both concepts, it also becomes clear that we are already committed to using the concept of 'becoming' as well, which Hegel argues is the first genuine and concrete thought, as well as the foundational concept for everything that is yet to come (ENCI § 88). We are, in a sense, forced to adopt the new category of 'becoming,' because any thought that tries to distinguish between 'being' and 'nothingness' will find itself sliding back and forth, from 'being' that becomes 'nothing,' and from 'nothing' that becomes 'being.' Another way to think about this is to think of 'becoming' as the unity of 'being' and 'non-being,' which emerges from the indeterminacy of the original contradiction.

But notice that, on Hegel's account, 'becoming' did not result from any supposed correlation between our concepts and an external, 'noumenal' world, nor did it just take its place among a fixed set of categories that constitute experience; Hegel's categories do not fit Kant's scheme. Rather, 'becoming' simply comes to light as we follow the dynamic contradiction between 'being' and 'nothingness.' For Hegel, the categories of the *Logic* are not transcendental or separate from the real world, and they do not exist only in the mind. The categories are articulated by human beings, and elaborated in human communities reflecting on their deepest values and interests, but humanity is part of nature, and nature is part of the world. So, Hegel concludes that since thought is a feature of the really existing world, then whatever 'logic' is distilled from thought will naturally show us the same structure that we find in any and every domain we investigate. And since nature and the universe are always changing and developing, and humanity is part of this dynamic whole, we should expect that the categories of the *Logic* will be similarly dynamic. Indeed, at the same moment that 'becoming' emerges, it also slips away, towards the concept of 'being-there,' which becomes 'quality,' and so on (ENCI §§ 89–91).

It may be that years after finishing the *Phenomenology*, Hegel changed his thinking about where exactly it fits in his 'system,' but it is at least an introduction to the *Logic* in the following sense: reading the *Phenomenology* requires a philosophical disposition that is serious and stalwart, but also adventurous and agile, and this is just the sort of intellectual disposition that will get one through Hegel's *Logic*. And this is not just a comment about the peculiar psychological attributes of people who read the *Phenomenology* and still want more; the point could be rephrased in terms of how well consciousness learns to think beyond the constraints of 'the understanding.' The distinction between 'subject' and 'object' is the most general opposition that is overcome on the way to 'absolute knowledge,' but it also happens to be the distinction that 'the understanding' clings to more jealously than any other. Hegel will have a lot to say about 'the understanding' in the *Logic*, and much of it will make little sense to someone who cannot think beyond its constraints.

ii. REASON AND 'THE UNDERSTANDING'

One fruitful way of representing the structure and development of the *Logic*, which happens to draw on some of the connections with the *Phenomenology*, is to cast 'the understanding' as the 'motor' of the unfolding dialectic. This interpretive angle also helps to clarify the relationship between philosophy and the social sciences, since Hegel argues that 'the understanding' characterizes the work of the empirical and social-scientific investigation. In Hegel's view, although 'the understanding' is an important and creative mode of thinking, it must be surpassed to some extent; we must understand its utility and limits in order to grasp what might lie beyond it (ENCI § 36, 82A).

The fundamental characteristic of 'the understanding' in Hegel's philosophy is that it reifies the relations between things, it grants to these relations a kind of 'objectivity' that tends towards becoming fixed and entrenched (ENCI § 6, 32A). In fact, 'the understanding' is even responsible for the 'things' that it relates, since they would not exist as discrete 'things' had 'the understanding' not artificially divided the whole into manageable parts to begin with. Many of the relations posited by the 'understanding' serve to organize our representations of the world, as in the case of the relations of cause and effect, or of universal and particular (ENCI § 20). The task for philosophy, as Hegel sees it, is to train the mind to pull away from our immediate representations, and away from the reifications of 'understanding,' not to leave them behind completely, but to grasp how their content might be preserved in the rich conceptual structure of the whole (ENCI § 1, 2, 5, 19, 80A).

It would be fair to describe the entire development of consciousness in the *Phenomenology* as the serial breakdown of the work of 'the understanding': each stage is surpassed when the forms of reification that characterize the mode of consciousness under consideration collapse, and 'the understanding' reliably fabricates another set of distinctions that launches the next stage. Most of the forms of reification are versions of the basic subject-object distinction, and consciousness reaches 'absolute knowledge' only when it abandons the last form of this basic distinction. Of course, these modes of consciousness are typically stubborn about their distinctions and reifications, since they offer interpretive power and security; they are only abandoned when, through immanent critique, they are brought to collapse and exhaustion. And we must remember that these modes of consciousness are not just vehicles for theories, but rather ways of living and being in the world; the path of the *Phenomenology* is indeed filled with suffering, labor, and despair.

But again, the negative characterization of 'the understanding' is only part of the story, and even in the *Phenomenology*, Hegel acknowledges its impressive power (PHG § 32). In the *Logic*, 'the understanding' plays a positive role in mediating the content that is taken up by the system of categories, and actively producing determinations of how these categories appear in the dynamic structure of the world (ENCI § 80A). One specific form of thinking that 'the understanding' issues forth is what Hegel calls in the Introduction to the *Encyclopedia* 'meditative thinking,' which is a kind of general reflection that occurs in the empirical sciences, and one that invites more philosophical thinking. This sort of reflection has two forms: (i) empirical or scientific meditative thinking that posits universal and particular, but without at the same time expressing a necessary connection between them, and (ii) speculative meditative thinking that tries to find these necessary connections. The latter type of meditative thinking is more truly philosophical, according to Hegel, and has the dialectic as its 'very nature' (ENCI § 9, 11). And while 'the understanding' is responsible for bringing thought into the system of categories, it is also indispensable for working in the other direction, as it relates universals to particulars in practical and theoretical spheres of discourse, for example, economics, political theory, jurisprudence, and sociology.

But how exactly does 'the understanding' make thought or thinking its object? And what exactly is its role in the dialectic, as the 'motor' of its development? Hegel attempts to answer these questions with some comments on the structure of the *Encyclopedia*

Logic, which occur just prior to the first main part (ENCI §§ 79–83). He begins by describing the *Logic* as having three sides or moments, 'the understanding,' 'the dialectical,' and 'the speculative,' and adds that all of the moments can be held together by 'the understanding,' but only in an artificial way (ENCI § 79). The first moment involves a familiar move of 'the understanding': in an act of abstraction, the whole is divided into parts and each part is taken to be self-sufficient and independent relative to the other parts. The second (dialectical) moment is also the work of 'the understanding,' but now it sees that the parts it just identified are not so independent after all, and in fact cannot be understood apart from their relations to other parts and the whole. The third moment, the speculative moment, introduces a new kind of explanation that resolves the inadequacies of the other moments: the relation that matters is the internal self-relation that exists between the whole and its parts, not the external relations of parts to other parts. These three moments can also be played out in the following way: a concept acquires a fixed meaning, that meaning is negated, and then a more complex concept emerges to contain both the original meaning and its negation.

Each of the categories taken up in the *Logic* represent categories that have historically been held by 'the understanding', that is, as doctrines that attempt to grasp reality through a fixed conceptual apparatus. When 'the understanding' seeks to grasp the whole through the use of a reified category, it meets with contradiction, because the 'whole' is not an unchanging thing that can be captured by fixed categories; it is more accurately thought of as a structured domain in which things pass in and out of existence. We can reconstruct this fluid and dynamic system of categories, but we should not take the categories to be the result of our own subjective intervention, of our individual 'understanding' diligently working with them. We must be careful here not to conflate the dynamic of the *Phenomenology* and the dynamic of the *Logic*. In the former case, the narrative develops from the point of view of a naïve consciousness that does not know where it is headed. In the latter case, though, the categories have already been fully developed through history, by the many forms of 'spirit' and their related forms of 'the understanding.' The system of concepts or categories in the *Logic* are reconstructed by us as we follow along, but were created by our predecessors long ago (ENCI § 88).

So, for example, in the move from 'being' to 'non-being' to 'becoming,' there is a sense in which pure thought has already made the move, but we readers of the *Logic* reconstruct this dynamic structure and thereby develop our ability to hang on to these abstract thoughts, and move within them, unburdened by the reifications of 'the understanding' (ENCI §§ 11, 19–20). There is even a kind of freedom that pure thought enjoys, because it is completely 'at home with itself,' and not positioning itself against an 'other'; and we experience this freedom insofar as we can train ourselves to dwell in this pure thought (ENCI §§ 20A, 23–4A). And Hegel thinks that this kind of training is useful in other areas of inquiry, because we come to know our thoughts as what they are, and therefore we come to understand our thinking about the state, history, law, 'ethical life,' and so on, at a much deeper level (ENCI §§ 19–20A, 24A).

iii. NECESSITY IN NATURE

In the *Philosophy of Nature* (the second part of the *Encyclopedia*), Hegel tries to articulate the ultimate conceptual structure of nature, from the categories of space and matter, through chemistry, biology, and ultimately to the emergence of life. He is particularly interested in the mechanical, chemical, and organic systems that emerge when the structure of nature is studied, and he wants his account to fit all of our empirical and scientific observations of nature. Though some of the specific theories of chemical and organic processes that Hegel endorsed have come to be discredited in the twentieth century, his thinking at the time was based on his extensive familiarity with the best science available to him, and was reasonable enough when judged by that standard. The main distinction Hegel seeks to preserve as he lays out his philosophy of nature is between a genuinely philosophical approach to nature, and an empirical or natural-scientific approach. He argues that while both forms of inquiry are systematic, the task of a philosophical approach is to explain necessity in nature, to capture the changes and transformations in the natural world that reveal the structure, or, as he calls it, the 'rationality,' of nature. The account of nature that emerges here will be an *a priori* account, not a set of generalizations that fall out of empirical observation.

But although his approach to studying nature is different, Hegel does not think his view is in direct competition with contemporary scientific thinking, and moreover, he thinks that the philosopher of nature must have more than a casual interest in the findings of empirical science. He does not want to fall into the philosophers' trap of starting with *a priori* reflection, developing a view of the rational structure of nature, and only then, as an afterthought, taking an interest in the findings of empirical science. At that point, with an *a priori* account already worked out, one would be tempted to embrace only those empirical findings that confirm it, and to ignore or dismiss any that do not (ENCII § 246R). Any philosophy of nature that routinely falls into this self-serving trap might be described as a 'strong *a priori*' account, and though Hegel does seem to suggest it at times, there is much more textual evidence in support of a different view, one that is committed to a weaker conception of the *a priori* in nature. According to this 'weak *a priori*' view, the philosopher of nature is very interested in what empirical science discovers, but has the aim of pulling away from the empirical data as soon as possible to start reconstructing it by way of *a priori* reflection, to show how everything fits together with some sort of necessity and systematicity. In the end, the scientist and the philosopher should end up on the same page, but they will have arrived there by different routes (ENCII § 246; ENCI § 12R).

Hegel's writings show that he took very seriously the findings of the leading scientists of his day, and this supports the notion that he must be operating with the weaker version of the *a priori* argument. But he does pull away from what empirical observation warrants, and starts to develop his organic conception of nature, which he now sees as the way to move beyond both reductionist materialism and Kant's subjective idealism. Hegel uses the organic concept of nature to argue that matter and self-consciousness are both stages in the development of nature. The organic metaphor ultimately brings together our account of nature and the way nature really is, because they will have a shared structure that is contained by the organic whole. He thought that starting with the blunt opposition between 'our subjective experience' and 'the objective world as it really is' leads to an impasse, and so he takes a different approach. His early response to this basic Kantian dualism was influenced directly by Schelling and romanticism, but by the middle of his career, with a better sense of his own view, Hegel became concerned to show that the organic conception of nature could be elaborated in a rigorous and scientific manner.

But Hegel's move to embrace the organic whole does not so much engage Kant's arguments as it just avoids them and changes the subject. This may seem like an unwarranted evasive maneuver, but Hegel thinks that philosophy produces many such impasses, where engaging the arguments at hand is futile. A related type of impasse is produced by skepticism, and when Hegel considers it in the Introduction to the *Phenomenology*, his response is similar: he knows that the skeptic cannot be answered directly, utilizing the same one-sided concepts that give skepticism its force, so the only response is to change the subject, and move on with concepts that explain the skeptic's one-sidedness. Of course the skeptic will not recognize this as a legitimate response, but Hegel nonetheless invites us (if not the skeptic) to follow along, with the proviso that we will come to see the legitimacy of the move when we look backwards from the systematic and comprehensive point of view that he is developing. Likewise with the organic conception of nature, Hegel invites us to go along with him on the promise that eventually, when the whole view is on the table, we will be able to accept it.

Kant, of course, was not about to make that sort of move, and we can see very clearly what this refusal amounts to when we consider his treatment of teleology, which he calls 'natural purpose,' in the *Critique of Judgment* (CJ §§ 64–5, 67). Kant argues that teleology has two essential features: first, contrary to the mechanistic picture where the parts precede the whole, in the case of the organism with 'natural purpose,' the whole precedes the part; and second, the organism is self-guiding and self-organizing. But although Kant thinks that teleological judgements may be useful to systematize and complete our understanding of the physical world, their use must be limited; teleology must only be a 'regulative principle' for our reflection, and we are not warranted to read teleology into the nature of things (CJ § 67).

Hegel found Kant's analysis of teleology very useful, and appropriated it wholesale, with the modification that he thought you could read these properties into nature. And of course, Hegel struggled to show that the teleology one was warranted to read into nature had to be 'intrinsic' instead of 'extrinsic.' He was not interested in recruiting the external teleology of Christian theology or of vitalism, or in asserting that a self-organizing creature needed thereby to have a free will or self-consciousness. Hegel just wants to be able to talk about natural objects having functions, or proto-intentionality, as part of the necessary structural development of nature considered as a whole.

Hegel rejected the evolutionary theories of his day, because they lacked the resources to capture this 'internal' teleology, and so, he thought, could not offer genuine explanations of what is necessary in nature. Whether it was called 'evolution' (development from the lowest natural form to the highest) or 'emanation' (development from the most to the least perfect), and concerned epigenesis or preformation, Hegel took these to be gradual quantitative processes that were observed but not explained (ENCII § 249Z, 339Z2). Of course, some of Hegel's contemporaries thought that intrinsic teleology was observable and that you could see self-organization at work, but Hegel was unpersuaded (ENCII § 249Z). Capturing necessity at work in nature, Hegel insisted, required that one develop an *a priori* account.

Contemporary interpretations of convergent evolution seem to be the sort of account Hegel was looking for, because they are clearly dependent on an *a priori* explanation of the functional exigencies that generate similar adaptations in otherwise independent populations of organisms. The cases of convergent evolution are interesting because they make the distinction very neatly between what is contingent in nature, and what is necessary and systemic in nature. Living organisms often find themselves in conditions where they must either adapt to a certain environmental challenge or die. When similar environmental challenges exist in different times and places, nature always seems to come up with the same solution, and Hegel would interpret this as the assertion of natural necessity. So, for example, the basic structure of vision and the mechanics of the eye recur in a great variety of organisms across the natural world. These organisms share the same general evolutionary pressures, because they live in a lighted transparent medium, and they must move around to survive and reproduce. In these conditions, the typical form of vision ends up being highly effective and efficient for these organisms. Philosophers like Daniel Dennett and evolutionary biologists like Stuart Kauffman, are starting to reformulate the whole phenomenon of convergent evolution in terms of rules and organizing principles, which is exactly the language that Hegel would prefer. With this reformulation, the focus is not so much on the final adaptations that organisms acquire, but on the basic rules of design and principles of engineering that organisms seem to have adopted. And this is an expansion of Hegel's view of the internal teleology of organisms, such that now their self-organizing activities can be expressed as somewhat formal rules and principles.

Hegel is interested in the rationality or structure of nature, as it is reconstructed from layers of contingency, especially where that structure explains the 'forced moves' that organisms must make in order to survive. Although Hegel does not characterize it in this way, it might be helpful to consider whether there are other 'forced moves' in nature that have shaped the course of human history. For example, is language acquisition a 'forced move' for humans? Are some psychological or phenomenological states 'forced moves'? What about specific political arrangements in history? And is there a sequence of 'forced moves' that could be reconstructed? In Hegel's view, these questions pull us out of the domain of nature and into the domain of 'spirit,' where we do find an analogue to the 'forced moves' of nature, but one which takes on a qualitatively different shape because 'spirit' introduces self-awareness and interiority, which, he thinks, is not present in mere nature.

iv. THE EMERGENCE OF SPIRIT

Hegel's *Philosophy of Mind*, the third part of the *Encyclopedia*, shows how self-conscious 'spirit' gradually emerges from nature and becomes aware of itself; and since we humans are the ones whose activity becomes 'minded' or characterized by 'spirit,' and since we are also just as much part of nature as any other organism, the self-awareness of 'spirit' is also, in a sense, nature coming to know itself as nature. At this point in Hegel's system, it becomes easier to understand his distinctive brand of metaphysics, based on structure instead of substance, because one of the key points about 'spirit' is that it is not a 'thing'; rather, in Hegel's words: 'Spirit is what spirit does, and its deed is to make itself the object of its own consciousness' (PR § 343). Hegel also expands his thinking about 'spirit' in this part of the *Encyclopedia*, beyond the view of the *Phenomenology*, to include an account of individual human psychology as it emerges from nature and begins thinking, willing, and reflecting. This individual domain will become 'subjective spirit,' and will complete his overall scheme that also includes 'objective spirit,' the 'mindedness' of social groups, institutions, and states, and 'absolute spirit,' the highest order reflection on humanity's basic values and interests beyond to confines of any particular group or political state.

First and foremost, the translation of *Geist* is difficult, because it can mean 'mind' or 'spirit,' and even has some etymological connections with 'soul' and 'ghost'; but these translations are all misleading. It is better to think of *Geist* as 'mindedness' or 'spirituality,' since these are closer to Hegel's meaning, and avoid the heavy metaphysical connotations of the typical translations. This naturalized and demystified way of talking about 'spirit' also helps reveal its relationship to nature: there is nothing non-natural about 'spirit,' it is rather like an emergent property of nature that appears when the right sort of structure and complexity is in place. At some point in natural history, we humans acquired our sense of interiority and internal directedness, in small ways at first, but then gradually acquiring the ability to distance ourselves from the necessity of nature (ENCIII § 381). Mere matter, for Hegel, is explained by the 'external' principles of force, gravity, friction, and so on, and has a long way to go before it can support the emergence of 'spirit'; when 'spirit' does emerge, though, it becomes self-directing, and can be explained by its own 'internal' principles.

Our first self-distancing move, Hegel argues, took the form of habit: our natural mental state was scattered and entropic, and our awareness of sensations and feelings was rudimentary, but at some point our actions became habituated, which opened up a new possibility for us (ENCIII §§ 409–10). If one is habituated to behave in a certain way, then any sensations or feelings that arise during that behavior are pushed to the side and not immediately acted upon. This generates a basic awareness that one's sensations and feelings do not automatically determine one's actions, which then creates a space for conscious self-directedness. But Hegel emphasizes that this process is made up of small steps; the emergence of habit is something of a landmark, because it gives us a glimpse of being 'at home' with ourselves, but it is just one moment in a long and gradual developmental process (ENCIII § 410). There are even a number of necessary stages prior to habit that Hegel thinks we share with non-human animals, and that we recapitulate as children; he also thinks that we find echoes of these early stages in cases of insanity, and in our patterns of waking and sleeping (ENCIII § 398). Hegel also points out that while the emergence of 'spirit' is necessary, and so is bound to occur sometime and somewhere, the specific features of this emergence will depend on a number of contingent factors; in any case, he is less interested in the exact historical details than the overall phases of development.

A notable feature of this gradual process is its lack of transparency: individual human beings have very little awareness of what is going on when 'spirit' emerges from nature. Our intentions are generally not known to us, and certainly not before we reach a very high level of self-understanding and development; our awareness and understanding of such things exists on a continuum. This is an important feature of Hegel's account, because it positions him against Descartes and others who think that the workings of the mind are immediately transparent to us; Hegel's view is that subjectivity and interiority take root gradually, and that our understanding of agency and intention must develop accordingly. And since we are never entirely freed from the necessity of nature, we will always have to evaluate the effect of contingent causal influences on our intentions and actions.

We also find with the emergence of 'spirit' a large-scale application of Hegel's maxim, 'to lose oneself is to find oneself,' which emphasizes that 'spirit' is like an individual self, despite its diverse manifestations and many stages of development. This one 'spirit' is the 'minded' part of nature, and is a natural extension of Hegel's idea of organic unity and self-development: 'spirit' is like an organism with its own dynamic, self-directed, and goal-oriented behavior, and its goal is to know itself. So at first, we become aware of ourselves as creatures with interests and desires, which seem to be in opposition to nature; for example, our desire for food requires that we confront nature and eat it, and meanwhile, other creatures in nature are trying to eat us. But over time, we start to understand that the structure of our desires and interests is also manifest in other domains (in other creatures, at first, but also eventually we see these as patterns of pure thought); at that point, we 'lose ourselves' to nature, because what used to be 'our' experience now appears as a general feature of nature, our 'selves' have been dissolved in nature. But then we can come to find ourselves again after we acquire a full understanding of nature as a whole, and can now identify with its structure and be 'at home' in it. Our whole practice of scientific and philosophical inquiry into nature, then, reconstructs this self-directed and goal-oriented behaviour, and as we consider rival accounts of nature, we realize that nature already has to be a certain way to have produced creatures like us, who are now busily examining it, and struggling to be 'at home' in it.

Hegel's concept of 'spirit' is closely related to his notion of 'essence' or 'substance,' which he will ultimately use to designate the historically specific content of 'ethical life' in the *Philosophy of Right*. His term is *Wesen*, which means 'being,' 'essence,' 'substance,' or even quite generally, 'the nature of a thing,' and he often uses 'substantiality' and 'essence' interchangeably (PR § 145, 147, 153). But although Hegel uses traditional language here, his essentialism avoids the metaphysical baggage associated with, say, Aristotle's view in the *Nicomachean Ethics*. Hegel's essentialism might be described as an 'internal' or 'historicized' naturalism where this signifies an essence that varies across historical periods as well as across specific cultural and political communities, and that can only be articulated as a particular group's self-understanding. That one has an 'essence' or 'substance' does not vary across different cultures or historical periods; it is the content that varies. *Wesen* functions much like the weak claims that we are language using creatures, that we are social animals, or that we are creatures who have the capacity to take up various perspectives on a continuum from particular to universal. For Hegel, our 'essence' must be made determinate in our specific cultural, historical, and political surroundings; it cannot be formulated with any determinacy by reference to timeless and final truths about who we are as individuals. We are always in the process of formulating our own essence through history, and so the project of self-understanding will always be the project of trying to comprehend the age in which we live, and how we are able to articulate the concepts we use, the ideals we pursue, and the 'selfhoods' we embody.

Hegel thinks of 'ethical life' as 'Spirit living and present as a world' and the setting where 'spirit' begins to exist 'as Spirit' (PR § 151), and the 'substance' of 'ethical life' will be expressed by our collective interpretation of ourselves, our estimation of our most basic values and interests. It may seem impossible to capture this kind of 'self-understanding' of a cultural or political community, let alone an historical period, given the facts of heterogeneity and pluralism that tend to characterize even small groups; but Hegel does think it is possible to talk about this in terms of very general social aspirations. For example, in the *Philosophy of Right*, Hegel takes the 'essence' or 'substantiality' of humanity, as it exists in the fairly determinate context of the modern state, to be expressed in two seemingly opposed aspirations, towards autonomy, negative rights, and individuality on the one hand, and towards expressive wholeness, community, and solidarity on the other (PR §§ 22–32). There is also the very general 'substance' of what it is to be a human being living in the modern period, which, for Hegel, means that one will be concerned with making sure that our choices and ends are justifiable to us in terms that make no arbitrary appeals to authority. With this conception of *Wesen* in mind, it becomes easier to see that in Hegel's view, the self that is being realized is not one, but many. Hegel would consider it to be a kind of dogmatism to hold that only one kind of self-understanding, one self-identification, is sufficient for being free; his position is that modernity has placed on the table the possibility that individuals can have multiple identities, each of which is actualized through participation in organized institutional forms of activity.

And just as habit was an important first step in the emergence of 'subjective spirit,' it has a similar role in the emergence of 'objective spirit': it is only when a group is organized around specific norms that become internalized and habituated that 'objective spirit' is actualized. When one is habituated into the norms of a group, one distances oneself from any desires that run counter to these norms, and this allows one to embrace a social identity and selfhood that exists independently of one's personal self. And the content of these collectively shared norms will be the 'substance' of 'ethical life,' and will be supported by the institutions and practices of culture. On this view, the cultural institutions of *Bildung* will be essential to the dynamic stability of 'ethical life,' because they habituate us to act in accordance with 'objective rationality.' And 'absolute spirit' will involve communal reflection on the basic values and interests that support 'objective rationality' in this context, as well as the 'substance' of 'ethical life' in general. All of this goes by pretty quickly in the condensed prose of the *Encyclopedia*, but everything that appears in its third part, the *Philosophy of Mind*, under the rubric of 'objective spirit' gets a much more detailed treatment in the *Philosophy of Right*.

CHAPTER 5

THE *PHILOSOPHY OF RIGHT*: FREEDOM AS SELF-REALIZATION

When we hear it said that freedom in general consists in *being able to do as one pleases*, such an idea can only be taken to indicate a complete lack of intellectual culture; for it shows not the least awareness of what constitutes the will which is free in and for itself, or right, or ethics, etc. (PR § 15)

In 1959, a practically unknown jazz saxophonist named Ornette Coleman had a string of performances at a prominent jazz club in New York City, and immediately generated widespread controversy among critics, musicians, and audiences. Coleman's playing seemed to abandon harmonic structure, typical song-forms, and even many basic rhythmic conventions that had long been taken for granted; even his technique in playing the saxophone failed to conform to accepted standards. It would seem that Coleman was simply in pursuit of more freedom (as might be suggested by the title of his 1960 album, *Free Jazz*, which became the lasting name for this style of jazz), and we would expect his fellow jazz musicians enthusiastically to join in; but this was not the case. Other musicians reacted with a rather stunning amount of hostility, labelling him as a charlatan, and it is important to understand why.

A common view of jazz improvisation takes jazz musicians to be enjoying a desirable kind of freedom, namely the freedom to play 'whatever one feels like playing,' spontaneously and whimsically; this kind of freedom is considered desirable, even deeply liberating, and is an application of a common view of freedom in general, as 'being able to do whatever one wants to do.' On this view of free-dom, any kind of interference or constraint on what one wants to do will reduce one's freedom. Philosophers tend to call this view 'freedom as non-interference' or 'negative freedom.' But at some level, all jazz musicians have rejected the conception of freedom as non-interference, because they know that music occurs in a context of constraints, norms, and rules, but they see these forms of 'inter-ference' not as a limitation of their freedom, but rather as a struc-tured context in which freedom becomes meaningful. For example, any jazz ensemble will play in accordance with a structured set of rules that determine to some extent how musicians respond to the nomenclature of the sheet music. Even before the performance, the norms of harmony, rhythm, cadence, and notation were in effect for the composer who created the music, and improvising musi-cians, who are composing on the fly, engage this same normative structure.

Musicians, then, have at least implicitly rejected the conception of freedom as non-interference and replaced it with a conception of freedom as self-realization. Although the musician could choose to play any notes whatever, at any time whatever, he or she instead plays in accordance with the norms of music, which become enabl-ing conditions for self-realization. That is, the musician comes to identify with these restrictions, and to see them as self-imposed, by way of understanding that the whole idea of an ensemble supposes that a multiplicity of musicians can willingly limit and synchronize itself so as to produce music. For the musician, affirming and working with the rules of music and musical ensembles is a form of expressing oneself as a musician, the realization of musical selfhood. This process of affirming the structures that enable one to engage in self-realization is an act of taking responsibility, per-haps even a kind of heroic embrace, and can be described as a kind of 'reflective identification.' One externalizes one's will as it is projected into the structure of music, and internalizes that same structure into one's conception of self.

But if we stopped here, we might still worry about whether the norms, rules, and structures of music are the right ones. Could a different set of musical norms be 'better'? Are musicians really just submitting themselves to an arbitrary source of authority? And it is here that Hegel's theory of freedom has much to say, and can carry the analysis further. In his view, any normative structure that is taken to provide a context for self-realization must also be subject to evaluation by those acting within it. It is not enough that one follows the rules of a game if this is done without understanding why that game is a good one to play, or why those rules best express the fundamental aims of the game. This higher order evaluation demands that people be in a position to reinterpret the system of rules under which they seek self-realization and consider whether that system is coherent and consistent, and whether it can attain the goals it sets for itself.

In the case of the musician, Hegel would say that for such a person to be genuinely free, he or she must know the structure of harmony and composition, as well as all the norms governing improvisation, and also be in a position to influence and revise this system of rules if revision seems warranted. Hegel would argue that a musician must be in a position to articulate a view about what the institutions of music aim to achieve, what criteria they set for themselves, and whether the current set of rules and norms can work towards satisfying those criteria. This is not to say that a musician must be able to carry out this kind of evaluation in order to play well; it is to say that this musician will not be as free as possible without engaging in this kind of higher order evaluation and self-reflection.

In 1959, the question that most critics and musicians were asking about Ornette Coleman was this: why is he brazenly and flatly rejecting the normative structure of jazz? And their answer was that he must have deeply misunderstood the role of structure in jazz. The musicians were right to assert that structure is a condition for the possibility of freedom, but they had asked the wrong question about Coleman's music; Hegel's philosophy, though, allows us to ask the right question: was Coleman engaged in higher order reflection on the normative structure of jazz itself? It is fair to say, now looking backwards, that Coleman was indeed questioning the whole normative structure, and though we may disagree with his analysis, conclusions, or tactics, and we may not like his music, we should at least acknowledge that our disagreements are about the general aspirations of art. Far from being a charlatan, Coleman was engaged in deeply philosophical reflection, and Hegel's philosophy helps us see this.

In this chapter, I will consider Hegel's *Philosophy of Right*, which contains the full description and elaboration of his theory of freedom, stretching from the abstract nature of the free will to the fully concrete context of the modern state. I will be mainly concerned with explaining the following: (i) self-realization and 'ethical life,' (ii) identification and externalization, (iii) acting in accordance with reason, and (iv) *Bildung* and the *Korporation*. Recall that Hegel's speculative hermeneutics, when applied to political philosophy, aims to 'portray the state as an inherently rational entity.' This chapter focuses on the 'rationality' that Hegel sees in the modern state; the critical dimension of his speculative hermeneutic treatment of the state is explored in the next two chapters.

i. SELF-REALIZATION AND 'ETHICAL LIFE'

The *Philosophy of Right* (published in 1821) is Hegel's main work of political philosophy, and is a much expanded version of the material found in the third part of the *Encyclopedia*, the *Philosophy of Spirit* (published just a few years earlier). The book, and his lecture course on the same (delivered seven times between 1817 and 1831), develops a substantive theory of the modern constitutional and democratic state as the appropriate setting for freedom and 'ethical life.' In the context of the modern state, 'ethical life' represents the fullest realization of freedom that is possible for us moderns; it signifies the entire ensemble of social relations and institutions that articulate the sphere of freedom, and constitute the basic way of life of a community. When 'ethical life' is actualized by the modern state, he suggests, 'spirit' will have expressed itself fully (PR §§ 142–57). Hegel argues that in 'ethical life' the oppositions between autonomy, individuality, and self-creation on the one hand, and integration, solidarity, and community on the other, can be sufficiently reconciled; the various pathologies and malaises that characterize modernity can be avoided, because in 'ethical life' we can actually attain the ideal of freedom that we seek.

Modern 'ethical life' is a promising ideal, Hegel argues, because it captures what freedom must look like for a whole society of individuals, and shifts our thinking about reason and rational self-determination to the level of the social whole. In 'ethical life,' reason and rationality are embodied in social practices and institutions, which in turn generate the norms that guide our practical reasoning. We are already proficient at scrutinizing our own reasons, choices, and actions in our lives, but in 'ethical life,' we will be attuned to the social content of our reasons and reason-giving practices; we will have reconciled the differences between what counts as a reason for me, and what counts as a reason for us. In the *Philosophy of Right*, Hegel argues that 'ethical life' overcomes the contradictions associated with more individualistic theories of freedom, and resolves as well the problems generated from traditional ways of thinking about morality; the structure of the *Philosophy of Right* indicates the flow of this argument: 'abstract right,' the individualist view of freedom as non-interference, is superseded by 'morality,' which is then superseded by 'ethical life.'

The most basic and abstract way of thinking about freedom is in terms of possession and property, and this is characteristic of what Hegel calls 'abstract right.' On this view, which is closely related to both contemporary libertarianism and eighteenth century classical liberalism, we are free insofar as we can appropriate property. And our ability to acquire and hold property without the interference of others, on this view, is expressive of our individual desires and interests, and generates a kind of 'natural' right to property; and possessing property is ideally a way of guaranteeing the non-interference of others, since one has exclusive rights of control over one's property. But Hegel argues that although this manner of thinking captures some of our basic intuitions, it nonetheless runs into problems when we consider the inevitable violations of property rights that arise. In any society with private property, there will be cases of theft and coercion, which undermine the normative basis for property rights; but how, Hegel asks, will these cases of transgression be addressed? The determination of who is right, who is wrong, who is to be redressed, and who is to be punished, cannot be carried out within the narrow constraints of 'abstract right.' If freedom is just the relationship between what I want and what I own, there is no intelligible way to talk about the set of social conventions and moral obligations that naturally arise to support a system of property rights. If we try to take up an impartial view of how rights, conventions, and obligations work here, we find that we have left the perspective of 'abstract right' behind.

It turns out, Hegel argues, that we need the richer conceptual resources of 'morality' to sort out the problems that arise in 'abstract right'; 'morality' is the supersession of 'abstract right.' To solve the problems that arise when rights conflict, we need some general conception of our moral obligations to others that captures the whole set of rights that anyone can claim for themselves (beyond just property rights). At this point, though, freedom means more than it did in 'abstract right'; in the context of 'morality,' freedom requires that one only accept those moral principles, or moral 'goods,' that one accepts as 'one's own.' Hegel is here working with Kant's conception of the moral agent as free, rational, and obligated to act solely for the sake of moral duty; but Hegel also thought that Kantian morality was radically indeterminate, because the 'categorical imperative' is only effective at specifying what one should not do, and even then, any such determination needs to appropriate some sort of content to work with. So, on the one hand, Hegel wants to give Kant some credit for contributing to the idea that all moral agents have a right to act on 'conscience' (and who therefore should under no circumstance be subject to coercion or control); but on the other hand, Kant still shares some of the blame for the viewpoint of 'morality,' which simply lacks the conceptual resources to supply any content for people's moral reasoning.

But without any shared content for moral reasoning, we are left with a society characterized by tension, and a chaotically diverse set of views about what is right, good, justified, and so on. This is why 'ethical life' is needed, and why it counts as a supersession of 'morality': it supplies a shared set of norms and a general way of life that is justified as a condition for the possibility of all being free. But since Hegel wants to acknowledge that 'abstract right' and 'morality' both got something right, that they are partially preserved even as they are transcended, he includes private property and a substantive set of individual rights as features of 'ethical life.' The three main spheres of activity in 'ethical life' according to Hegel are the family, civil society, and the state, where each allows us to express essential features of our modern humanity, but where none is allowed to overshadow or trump the others.

One might suspect that Hegel's notion of 'ethical life' is animated by a nostalgia for the *polis* of fifth century BCE Athens; but Hegel is at pains to dissociate his view from this sort of nostalgic romanticism, and he clearly rejects the ancient conception of freedom in the *Phenomenology of Spirit*, the *Philosophy of History*, the *Lectures on the History of Philosophy*, and the *Philosophy of Right*. Hegel thought that critical reflection and detachment from one's social roles and identities were not available stances for the ancient Greeks; these practices of self-examination, and the strong notion of individualism that they presuppose, needed the institutional support of Roman society to develop fully. He also wants 'ethical life' to be possible for a modern state, so he is assuming that any modern society will be pluralistic and heterogeneous, full of conflict and dissent. And finally, Hegel consistently defends individual rights, and takes them to be central to 'ethical life'; individuals will always have the ability to abstract from their social roles, and must always be recognized to some extent as individuals (PR § 124, 185).

With the idea of 'ethical life' and the overall argument of the *Philosophy of Right* in mind, consider one of Hegel's key formulations of freedom, which we should now be able to unpack: freedom is 'being at home with oneself in one's other' (ENCI § 24A2; PR § 7A): The multiple layers of 'ethical life' suggest that what counts as one's 'other' here will depend on the context. We must think about what it means to 'be at home with oneself' regarding: our personal choices, actions, and ends; our social interaction with others, in various institutional and political contexts; and our place in history, nature, and the universe. If we consider the *Philosophy of Right* alongside the third part of the *Encyclopedia*, we should start to get a better sense for Hegel's threefold structure of freedom: 'subjective,' 'objective,' and 'absolute.' The question for Hegel becomes: what are the conditions for the possibility of identifying with one's self and one's actions in the world, in all of the relevant domains? The *Philosophy of Right* is mainly concerned with 'subjective' and 'objective' freedom, but it does establish that the state is a precondition for the exercise of 'absolute' freedom. At each level, if we are to be 'at home,' it is essential that we reflect on and understand what we are doing; for Hegel, freedom resides both in action and in the knowledge that that action is expressive of freedom (PR §§ 142, 146–7, 152, 257–8, 260, 268).

'Subjective freedom' requires that one identify with one's actions and ends, and this will typically involve some feeling of independence, self-directedness, and autonomy. One should be able easily to generate reasons for those actions and ends, reasons that flow from one's preferences, desires, and such. The identification that characterizes subjective freedom is obviously undermined by external or arbitrary coercion, but it can also be undermined by internal forces like the desires or drives that fuel addiction and interfere with those projects one takes to be authentic and expressive of the true self (ENCIII § 475R). 'Objective freedom' involves the externalization of our will, which brings into relief the many ways our actions and ends are mediated by others. Our life's projects, for example, are obviously mediated by our social, political, and historical setting, since we can only choose from among options available to us, and since many of the core values that influence these choices are handed down to us in our native cultures. Even the reasons we use to justify our choices to ourselves are implicitly aimed at others; at the level of 'objective freedom,' the cultural and institutional influences on our use of reasons is brought into relief. Hegel calls the highest level of freedom 'absolute,' and it requires that we cultivate our ability to understand the broadest possible matrix of relations mediating our actions and ends. This includes the mediations of history, nature, and the deep structure of the universe. Understanding these mediations is often complex and difficult, and it is perhaps even more difficult to reintegrate one's findings into one's general self-understanding. The sort of reflection that characterizes 'absolute freedom' is carried out in the domains of art, religion, and philosophy.

Hegel's theory of freedom is best characterized as a theory of 'rational self-realization': at the same time that we come to know and be ourselves, we are also projecting or externalizing ourselves into the world, and reintegrating the world back into ourselves. This double movement is important, since it suggests that it would not be sufficient for the will to be merely expressive: for Hegel, freedom is not just 'being with oneself' but 'being with oneself in the other' (PR § 5). We are supposed to seek, Hegel argues, a kind of mediated identity between ourselves and the world, and we do this through the use of reason. And for Hegel, as we know, reason and rationality are essentially social, so the mediated identity that we seek will require that we internalize the rationality and structure of 'ethical life.'

As a final comment, consider the breadth and ambition of Hegelian freedom: it is intended to be broad and deep, even at the cost of sounding unwieldy, impractical, and impossible to utilize in a workable political theory. It is certainly broader than the conception of freedom as non-interference ('negative' freedom) familiar to contemporary libertarians, and it does not quite fit the contours of so-called 'communitarian' ('positive') freedom. It resists characterization as either 'negative' or 'positive' since it tries to capture features of both; the conditions for Hegelian freedom are established in a matrix of social relations that allow for some degree of non-interference as well as relations of positive identification. Indeed, Hegel's aspiration was to provide a positive vision of human social and political life such that many of the oppositions that have re-emerged in recent political philosophy, between the freedoms of 'the ancients' and of 'the moderns,' between communitarians and liberals, and between individualism and holism, could be overcome.

ii. IDENTIFICATION AND EXTERNALIZATION

'Subjective' freedom is largely characterized by the process of identification, and since Hegel thinks that this must include a certain level of understanding and awareness, it is best described as a kind of 'reflective identification.' According to Hegel, modern individuals take themselves to have the unlimited ability to abstract from the roles they find themselves in, but also the unlimited ability to identify with these roles; one only becomes free and self-realizing through the affirmation of both the determinacy of identification and the indeterminacy of abstraction at the same time, and each associated ability is exercised in reflective identification. Hegel argues that reflective identification has three moments: (i) one abstracts from any roles or identifications, imagining endless possibilities of willing, (ii) one 'determines,' or imagines, oneself in a determinate role or identity, and (iii) one acknowledges these first two moments, but sees neither as definitive, and consciously embraces the action or end in question (PR §§ 4–10, 14; PHG § 177). Reflective identification, then, is all three moments taken together, which should assert the identity between self and action.

The first moment of reflective identification shares the basic contours of Kant's theory of freedom as rational self-determination, where the task is to abstract from all contingent or 'heteronomous' sources of willing, so as to act for the sake of duty alone; but there are reasons to resist any assimilation to Kant's theory. First of all, although Hegel's starting point is the assumption of the free and capricious will, this is an historical point for him, not a metaphysical one, as it is for Kant: on Hegel's view, we moderns have come to interpret ourselves as having a free and autonomous will, and this has been sufficient to develop our capacity to reflect on our ends and abstract from our roles and identities (LHPI pp. 29–48). Also, Kant imagines a strict opposition between reason and passion, but Hegel rejects this idea because it yields a conception of the self as bifurcated and alienated. Third, reason for Kant is universal and formal, but for Hegel, reason unfolds in history, and must be embodied by social and institutional structures (LHPI pp. 49–54). Finally, for Hegel, selfhood is intersubjectively mediated, which radically refashions the entire model of self-determination, and introduces a kind of self-distancing and ambiguity that have no place in Kant's view.

The most important part of reflective identification is the third moment, which represents a qualitative break from the familiar voluntarist model of self-determination and autonomy. This qualitative break is a supersession of the standpoint of the radically independent will, a move that demands a different way of talking about our sense of having an independent will, a way of talking that admits of a certain humility and ambiguity. Hegel argues that the ability to think of oneself as a 'person,' as an abstraction, is in a sense the greatest achievement of humanity at the same time that it has a contemptuous narrowness to it: no other animal in the natural world, nor any other human prior to modernity, could embrace the paradox of this abstract person (PR § 35). Reflective identification, then, is actually a kind of heroic embrace of this paradox: one is aware of one's ability to abstract, and knows that this abstraction is predicated on a myth, but then also affirms one's choices, actions, and ends, with all of their contingency and ambiguity.

The second part of Hegelian freedom, 'objective freedom,' requires that one externalize one's will, as part of the overall effort to establish a mediated unity between 'self' and world. This means that one must understand the 'objective' normative structures (institutions) in which we formulate and carry out our actions and ends. In order to feel 'at home with oneself' in this institutional context, one must identify with and embrace these structures as expressive of who and what one is. There is a double movement here, of externalization and internalization: one's actions and ends are brought 'out of' oneself into the world, and then the mediations revealed by that externalization are then brought 'back into' one's self, in a process of internalization. This means that the 'self' undergoes change as this mediated unity is established, and so also, that the 'self' is more the result than the starting point of freedom.

When Hegel analyzes the free will in the Introduction to the *Philosophy of Right*, and specifies its three moments (the three moments of 'reflective identification'), it is significant that this structure mirrors the moments of Hegel's account of pure recognition in the *Phenomenology* (PR § 7A). Both accounts start with a narrowly egoistic self that sees others as a threat to its independence, but then show that this moment is superseded by a self that knows that the path to independence is through dependence. Of course, the *Philosophy of Right* is a different context in which to consider pure recognition: whereas the *Phenomenology* charts the experience of consciousness first on an individual level, and then historically through Christianity and finally to 'absolute knowledge,' it does not address the modern state, which is the subject of the *Philosophy of Right*. Relations of mutual recognition are never stabilized politically in the narrative of the *Phenomenology*, but in the modern state, assuming it is rational, relations of mutual recognition already exist, and so there is no need for anyone to relive the struggle for recognition in the sense of the master-slave dialectic (ENCIII § 432A). 'Abstract right' had considered freedom in terms of subjective independence, but now, if Hegel's theory of pure recognition holds, we must embrace the paradoxical implication that genuine independence requires dependence, that one cannot be free alone. This shifts the entire discussion of the kinds of reasons one has for choosing actions and ends since the whole idea of individual deliberation is now enriched with the conceptual argument that one only becomes 'an individual' by understanding that the independence of individuality is a kind of dependence.

The return of pure recognition here suggests a helpful characterization of 'ethical life,' as the stabilized and institutionally supported system of pure recognition, including all forms of recognition in the domains of the family, civil society, and the state. Of course, not all forms of recognition across these domains are identical, so one must imagine how they fall on a continuum from external and partial to developmental and complete. When one acts as an individual in civil society, exchanging goods, entering into contracts, and so on, one enjoys a kind of recognition; this kind of recognition is thin and external, but it confers upon anyone in civil society the status of a person with rights, who can raise claims against some kinds of interference and exploit some kinds of affordages. Indeed, this external and partial recognition is closely tied with what Hegel sees as the primary function of civil society, as a sphere of interaction in which individuality can fully develop.

Hegel argues that civil society, and the free competitive market that is its basis, is an indispensable sphere of human interaction precisely because it facilitates the free development of the individual and brings together (ideally) the particularity of the individual's interests with the universality of the entire ensemble of interests in society. It is the former function, the facilitation of bourgeois freedom, which is primary and most obvious for the agents who interact in civil society; the latter function, the coalescence of the particular and the universal, occurs initially 'behind the backs' of agents and only becomes a conscious influence in guiding behavior after the individual has been educated and acculturated towards a broader perspective through a process of *Bildung*. Hegel makes it clear that the kind of freedom developed and fostered in civil society is specifically modern: subjective freedom was originally perceived as a threat to the Greek state, developed in a religious context in Christianity, and only brought to its first imperfect political manifestation in the French Revolution. Civil society is part of 'ethical life,' but the antagonistic and individualistically oriented interests of this market based economic sphere cannot be allowed to undermine other central interests that exist in the functional balance of 'ethical life' (PR § 185).

Primarily then, civil society preserves the specifically modern freedom that is embodied by the individual who engages in the exchange of commodities and who, *ipso facto*, acts in accordance with norms of exchange (PR §§ 217–18). At this very basic level, Hegel is interested in the activity of the individual in civil society insofar as he or she dispenses of alienable property, money, labor, or goods, in exchange for other commodities. This is important for Hegel not because it is an intrinsic good that we all have the broad variety of commodities society has to offer, but because the property a person owns is an expression of our free will, and because we can exchange properties that we own for the properties of others. This exchange is, then, an act of pure recognition, in which we see the other as an individual with a free will and alienable property. At this point, individuals who exchange goods do not fully recognize each other, in the sense of each of the three moments of pure recognition; they rather embody the perspective of the rational egoist, and from this point of view are pulled necessarily into interaction with other like-minded individuals, and must recognize them as being the same. What Hegel wants from this is the establishment of minimal norms of exchange, that is, the entire collection of norms that regulate the behaviors surrounding the exchange of commodities and that are intelligible given the fact that these interactions are partial acts of mutual recognition. These norms are universal because they ignore the particularity of individuals and develop merely from the exchange relations that are established between individuals (PR § 182).

Hegel's idea is that individuals in modern society act in various domains, and so must be legally recognized as persons, subjects, and individuals. A developed system of law aspires to recognize each and all of these various selfhoods, which, when taken as a whole, amounts to a system of relations that is expressive of mutual recognition. And since law is dynamic, it is subject to ongoing reform as our communal understanding of our constantly evolving selves develops. For Hegel, the free individual is one who no longer sees the project of gaining some certainty about his or her actions and ends as one that is carried out alone. One learns though mutual recognition that the best hope one has for becoming free, for being at home with oneself, is with other individuals who can freely grant the status of agency and responsibility to each other. Moreover, if an individual lives in the context of the modern state, with 'ethical life' being realized to some extent or other, he or she will already exist in relations of recognition to some extent.

iii. ACTING IN ACCORDANCE WITH REASON

The third element of Hegelian freedom, 'absolute' freedom, involves our coming to understand and embrace the widest possible normative structure that mediates our actions and ends. At this level of contemplating our freedom, we are trying to internalize the 'reason' or basic organizing principles of the world, and this will appear, for Hegel, as a kind of broad practical rationality that will recursively shape the way we think about the other moments of freedom ('subjective' and 'objective'). Hegel's theory of freedom as self-realization rests on an ethical rationalism that is tightly linked to the way rationality is expressed by social structures that are ultimately shaped by communal self-reflection (PR §§ 28, 145). This will be important at the level of our political choices and engagements, but also at the level of our reflections in art, religion, and philosophy, the domains of 'absolute spirit.'

According to Hegel, acting freely means acting in accordance with reason, and this way of putting it is significant: 'acting in accordance with reason' captures better then the locution 'acting rationally' that one not only acts on reasons one takes to be 'one's own,' but also that these reasons are in accordance with objectively existing social structures that serve to validate these reasons and provide the context in which one translates these reasons into action. Acting in accordance with reason, then, cannot be reduced to the correct exercise of a faculty of mind; it is rather a way of living that fits in with the structure of some sphere of activity or other. Although Hegel thinks that freedom does entail a certain kind of reason-giving practice, he does not think that this practice can be described solely in terms of individual rational scrutiny; it must be taken to involve participation in and engagement with modern social and political institutions.

If a person is to be free when acting in accordance with a norm, that person must be able to identify with that action, and this raises the issue of what sorts of reasons a person has when deliberating about actions and ends, and whether these reasons are generated from established social norms. And this focus on the sorts of reasons a person has for action and for choosing ends is a natural development of the model of reflective identification considered earlier, for reflective identification is, in addition to being an activity of imaginatively considering various abstractions and determinations, is also a space of reasons. Hegel's emphasis on the rationality that is expressed by objective social structures is part of his view about how certain kinds of reasons come to be seen as good reasons for us, as reasons that have a certain authority. The idea of acting in accordance with reason, then, signifies the dynamic coalescence of reflective identification and the wide normative structure of society, which rests of course on the ambitious promise that such a coalescence is possible; this promise is, for Hegel, the promise of a higher form of practical rationality, one that expresses a greater dignity than rationality that is merely subjective or instrumental.

In Hegel's view, there are types of rationality that correlate to types of freedom, so in addition to the threefold distinctions already mentioned, we can add 'subjective,' 'objective,' and 'absolute' rationality. Subjective rationality is the sphere of an individual's reasons for engaging in actions, choices and ends, especially where these reasons are instrumentally related to that individual's narrow interests, desires, and preferences (PR §§ 146–7). The rationality of groups, institutions, and political states, are all forms of objective rationality, and are structured by reasons that have force issuing from the norms governing group activity (PR §§ 144–5). Minimally, objective rationality is the rationality of games, the structure of the organized behaviour of groups of people, which in a straight-forward sense is a more generalized type of activity than in the case of a single person acting alone. Hegel distinguishes, then, between a person acting on reasons that only have meaning for that person alone, and a person acting in the context of a game, where there is a plurality of individuals acting on reasons that have force in the context of a game. And what is 'objective' here has both the meaning that it actually exists, as the world that a person confronts and that has a certain permanence and indissolubility about it, and that it has a kind of validity that is broader than an individual's merely subjective point of view. Objective rationality is objective in the sense that the institutions from which it issues are greater than any individual will, exist before an individual will and individual identity comes to exist in them, and yet also supported by subjective rationality, since institutions are produced and reproduced by individual action and subjective reasons (PR § 142). 'Absolute' rationality will involve a type of reflection that is more general than what we find in 'objective' rationality: if objective rationality is the rationality of games, the reasoning that goes on within the normative structure of a game, then 'absolute' rationality takes step back and reflects on the general aim of a game, or the reasons why anyone plays games in the first place. In the case of the musician, Hegel would say that for such a person to be genuinely free, he or she must know the structure of harmony and composition, as well as the norms governing behavior in and around the performance, and also be in a position to influence and revise this system of rules if revision seems warranted (PR § 255, 315). To move from 'objective' to 'absolute' rationality in the domain of music requires that one be in a position to articulate a view about what the institutions of music aim to achieve, what criteria they set for themselves, and to ask whether the current set of rules and norms can work towards promoting those criteria.

Acting in accordance with reason will draw on our ability to self-consciously follow norms that we take as self-expressive, through which actions can be 'our own. This is why acting according to our various arbitrary desires and whims is often unsatisfying, that is, because we cannot take ourselves to be acting in accordance with reason in any way that actualizes an interesting kind of selfhood; in such cases, we cannot pretend that these actions have meaning at any level beyond ourselves (PR §§ 20–1). This introduces a level of justification or qualification for an individual's actions and ends that pulls one away from self-referential atomism: there must be a context in which we can link up our inclinations, desires, and projects, and this context cannot even be approached if one's frame of reference does not extend beyond one's will.

It is often the case that one merely notices that one has or is having a certain desire, but if one is to be free, one must make such a desire one's own by considering the ends that the desire aims at, and asking whether those ends are ones that can in fact be identified with, that are self-expressive. Hegel's argument here that 'merely natural' desires should be transcended will sound familiar, but although it resembles the typical rationalistic rejection of the body and its concomitant presumption of dualism, he does not mean that they are to be rejected in all cases; his point is that they tend to preclude or at least discourage an individual from taking up the sort of generalized perspective that can make values, commitments, and projects coherent such that self-realization takes place. Nor are 'natural' desires to be bluntly rejected in any strong sense, as one finds in the Kantian or Christian view of a struggle with one's desires and impulses; Hegel argues that desire is to be transcended, absorbed, elevated, and purified, but not flatly negated.

Our actions extend into a web of social relations, and so, we must be able to see a conjunction between what we value and the values embodied in social institutions if we are to 'be with ourselves' in our actions and roles defined by social relations (PR § 153). For Hegel, individuals have the capacity to abstract from all self-determinations and identifications as well as the capacity to identify with any specific sort of content or commitment, and the crucial moment is the third one, where the individual takes up both the indeterminacy of abstraction and the determinacy of identification, and yet ends up identifying with a content, seeing it as 'one's own,' expressed in the real, objective and concrete social conditions in which one finds oneself. And again, the point here is not just that there must be a concrete context in which one is to be free, but that after one sees his or her freedom as actual in the world, one reflectively reintegrates the objective ends of the social world into one's self (PR §§ 8, 9–10). If our freedom is really to become actual in the world, we have to understand how our freedom can extend into the world, and then internalize that social structure, make it part of ourselves. To the extent that we do this, the external is not seen as a threat or limitation; we can act in it in a fully self-determined way (PR §§ 22–4). One must, then, be able decipher the degrees of relation between one's various actions, ends, and projects, because, presumably, there is much more going on with a person than just his or her fleeting whims and desires, namely, an entire set of values, projects, plans, ends, commitments, and so forth, which are formulated, carried out, and made real in a specific historical situation that gives that person's projects and values content and provides a medium in which these various actions and ends relate to each other. Since a person's self is complex, there is only a minimal sense in which the simplicity of an arbitrary exercise of will could be self-realizing and a case of freedom (PR § 15). If a person is at all serious about understanding how his or her actions and ends are possibly self-realizing, then the extent to which these actions and ends are related to each other to form a coherent web will be paramount.

So, according to Hegel, just how contemplative, informed, and insightful does one have to be to experience freedom to the fullest extent? It may seem as though one must be near omniscient to be in a position to survey and evaluate the way all the different levels of rationality in society function and relate, and to be able to consider the way all of our actions and projects fit into this complex whole. First of all, it must be admitted that Hegelian freedom is more demanding in this sense than most commonly held conceptions of freedom: one must have a fairly sophisticated understanding of what one is doing, why one should be doing that, and how what one does fits into and expresses one's self-identity (PR § 15). But, of course, Hegel does not think that people are or can be this reflective all the time, which is why he recognizes the importance of habit. Like Aristotle, Hegel thinks that habit is philosophically significant, e.g., he thinks that the task of education is to show people how they can internalize ethical behaviours such that they become habitual, but he distinguishes between habit that is supported by reflection and habit that is detached from reflection; when people act habitually all the time, never entering into reflection, they suffer a kind of 'mental death' (PR §§ 151A, 268). Hegelian freedom, then, admits of varying degrees, where one is most free when being as reflective as possible; but this does not imply that one is supposed to aim to be as thoroughly wrapped up in knowledge or reflection all the time to the greatest extent possible, because in Hegel's view, we are always led back to action, engagement, and practical involvement with the world.

iv. *BILDUNG* AND THE *KORPORATION*

If the modern state is to express 'ethical life,' it must ensure that there are conditions in which everyone can engage in activity that is in accordance with 'subjective,' 'objective,' and 'absolute' rationality, and it must offer a coherent vision of how these domains of actions can coexist in some kind of functional and enduring harmony. Most generally, the state must be a place in which individuals can be 'at home' with themselves and their choices, actions, and ends. A rational state ensures that there are a variety of projects available for people to identify with, and these projects cannot contradict collective projects that are aimed at the general good (PR § 281). One of the state's responsibilities, then, is to support the institutional structure that promotes the proper acculturation so that citizens can see themselves as part of this coherent system: the state must support *Bildung*.

The account of *Bildung* in the *Phenomenology of Spirit* tries to show that the strategies of identification individuals are likely to employ will fail without a determinate conception of the common good, and the legal, economic, and political institutions of the modern state. In the *Philosophy of Right*, Hegel argues that there is an institutional framework within which such strategies will succeed, namely, the framework of 'ethical life,' which includes the spheres of the family, civil society, and the state. It is in the sphere of civil society that individuals deploy strategies of identification that can bridge the gulf between narrow egoism and the broad practical rationality Hegel advocates as the path to genuine freedom. In civil society, the individual can learn to identify with interests that transcend his or her own in two ways: through the facts of necessary cooperation required by the free market, and through participation in voluntary associations that Hegel calls 'corporations' (*Korporationen*).

Hegel makes the point (repeated decades later by Karl Marx in *Das Kapital*) that part of the individual's education in civil society can occur without any particular awareness or conscious deliberation: even the most egoistic and narrowly self-interested person will come to see that his or her actions become intertwined with the actions of everyone else, and so will begin to understand that an exclusive preoccupation with one's narrow ends will be self-defeating (PR §§ 182–3, 186–7). As Hegel sees it, all human needs, insofar as they arise and can be satisfied in the context of the modern state, are mediated by social institutions. They clearly have some natural origin, but by the time they are articulated in the market, through voluntary associations or public opinion, the purely natural is all but left behind. Any semblance of such needs being purely egoistic is left behind as well, since the various mediations of the formation and satisfaction of needs necessarily entail the activities of others on a fairly broad scale (PR § 184). This occurs particularly through work: in order to satisfy our needs, we must work to process natural resources, so work affects our theoretical and practical education, where the latter necessitates that we limit and control our activities so that they are appropriate (PR §§ 196–8).

The background for these realizations is the free market, which Hegel thinks has a certain attractive rationality to it when it functions at its best: each individual pursues his or her own interests, in the context of the variegated buying and selling of labor and commodities, and the more individuals act in their own interests, the more they serve the interests of the whole (PR § 199). The market mechanism (ideally) rationally allocates goods such that an aggregate of active particular interests is satisfied to the extent that each particular interest is pursued in its sphere of operation. This complex interaction of pursued interests would presumably offer, as well, a sufficiently varied context in which individuals can pursue a great variety of projects. At the same time that these particular interests are pursued, Hegel points out that they are brought into relation with each other: when the activity of an individual in the market, producing or purchasing goods, serves the interests of others, this is a kind of universality (PR § 181). Individuals who are at least moderately reflective will, then, have to think about the way their interests relate to others and how the aggregate of interests in the market functions as a whole; this realization is not sufficient for individuals to take up Hegelian practical rationality, but it is a necessary precursor.

The second kind of education in civil society, the more robust form, is the individual's activity in the *Korporation*, and here it is helpful to use the German term instead of its typical translation, 'corporation,' because it is crucial not to confuse it with the narrower idea of the business corporation; in German, a for-profit limited liability corporation is a *Koerperschaft*, not a *Korporation*. In Hegel's view, a *Korporation* is a voluntary association that functions as a kind of 'second family,' in that it looks after the welfare of its members in the face of the contingencies of the market, and so is the return of the ethical dimension to civil society, the sphere of activity in which the ethical is initially lost (PR §§ 249, 252, 255). The *Korporation* is also obligated to recruit and train its members, and to construct some procedure for certifying who is a member in full standing. The *Korporation* is also the primary context for the education of individuals from the particularity of their interests to the broader interests of their association (PR § 187). Because one takes pride in one's *Korporation*, as the body that represents the interests of one's trade or commonly shared ground project, the tendency to fall into a 'rabble mentality,' whether in the form of a poor or wealthy disposition, is greatly attenuated (PR § 253). So, for example, if one were a musician, and joined the musicians' *Korporation*, one would then see oneself not merely as a single laborer negotiating contracts and wages in the market, but as a tradesperson who, among all others of the same trade, works to make a living and is a valuable part of the commercial sphere of society.

When an individual is educated through membership in a *Korporation*, she or he gradually begins to integrate narrow individual interests with the more general interests of the *Korporation*. That is, though one can be motivated to join and work through a *Korporation* simply because one sees the personal advantages of mutual dependence and collective strength, since the corporation is also oriented by broader interests, and thus integrates such broad interests into its own workings, the individual comes to realize that his or her narrow interests are deeply connected with collective ones. Such developed conceptions of social self-identity acquired through participation in a 'corporation' would presumably motivate people to make different kinds of decisions regarding consumption, production and distribution as well.

But notice how this fits the model of self-sacrifice laid out in the 'self-alienated spirit' section of the *Phenomenology*. In that account, the initial atomistic consciousness had to be negated, and the same thing must happen here in civil society. When one first enters the sphere of civil society, one is narrowly interested in one's own welfare. But participation in a *Korporation* shows the individual that his or her narrow interests are illusory; the self that clings jealously to such narrow interests must be sacrificed. This presumably occurs as members of the *Korporation* take on the norms and disciplines of the group in regulating their behavior in ways that do not seem to be in their immediate narrow interest, or, to pick a dramatic example, in the case of a strike, where members of a laborers' *Korporation* risk their immediate individual well-being for the sake of the group. Also like the *Phenomenology* account, this kind of sacrifice has the double effect that when members of a corporation sacrifice their narrow interests, the group's collective power is made more actual, more real.

One can also see how activity in a corporation is an expression of pure recognition. Recall from the *Phenomenology* account of pure recognition, there are three moments: one loses one's abstract atomicity in recognizing the other as an identical being, one tries for self-recovery in soliciting acknowledgment from the other, and finally, both participants recover self-consciousness through mutual recognition. All three moments should occur through participation in a Hegelian *Korporation*. Members no longer see themselves as autonomous units grasping for power and wealth in market conditions, they instead recognize all the other members of their *Korporation* as individuals just like them. And yet, all of the members are not identical, since there is presumably some heterogeneity and structural differentiation in the group. Most importantly, members share bonds of solidarity, and acknowledgment from each other, which holds the group's interests together in crisis or adversity.

The *Korporation* in civil society serves as an important intermediate sphere of the education of the will, the primary institutional mediation of *Bildung*. To become a *gebildete* person, one does not need to move straight from egoism to a completely universal perspective more appropriate to the state. It will be remembered that this is one of the failed strategies from the *Phenomenology* account. The distinction between civil society and the state in Hegel's ethical life allows that this gradual educational process can take place. The way this educative process functions also shows why a truly universal perspective must be taken up by the state: if civil society educates citizens towards taking up a near-universal point of view, then a state is necessary to complete this progression.

Finally, in Hegel's view, the person who has properly undergone the process of *Bildung* does not attain a timeless, unmediated, and fully universal point of view; any such 'view from nowhere' is politically suspect and potentially self-delusional. The view that one eventually acquires is historically and culturally conditioned, and gradually takes shape through participation in a *Korporation*: individuals work towards a universal end within a corporation (PR § 264). The move towards an increasingly general perspective is embodied by the very structure of civil society and the state: the structure of 'ethical life' indicates the structure of rationality.

A 'universal' perspective here is a generalized one, and it entails all the concreteness of *Bildung* in the context of social practices and institutions (LNR § 91). At this point, Hegel's account comes full circle: one is free when one can identify with one's actions and ends, where these are taken to be conceptually tied to other individuals in determinate social, political, and historical contexts, and where one comes to understand and embrace through these actions and ends the wider structured context that mediates them.

CHAPTER 6

THE PHILOSOPHY OF HISTORY: REASON RULES THE WORLD

The only thought which philosophy brings with it is the simple idea of reason – the idea that reason governs the world and that world history is therefore a rational process. (PH 9)

A quick survey of the world's peoples and nations will reveal a staggeringly unequal distribution of wealth and power, and most indices of health, longevity, education, equality, freedom, and such, will be correlated to this distribution. At the same time that some countries have advanced medical technologies, overwhelming military power, and a dominating influence on the world's affairs, other countries have none of these, and have almost no chance of acquiring them. Consider the case of New Guinea, the large island just north of Australia; from the last ice age (about 14,000 years ago) until the end of the nineteenth century, the people of New Guinea experienced very little cultural and technological development. Just prior to the beginning of European colonization, New Guineans were essentially hunter-gatherers, using bows and arrows, pottery, and stone tools. The New Guinean highlands supported some agriculture, but no crops that were high in protein. Their political structure was tribal and based on small villages, and they were non-literate. And at the end of the nineteenth century, most Europeans and Americans considered New Guinea to be 'backwards' or 'primitive.'

Various explanations for this unequal distribution of wealth and power have been offered in the last couple of centuries, and most of these have implicitly or explicitly suggested that people in places like New Guinea must have lacked some set of skills, aptitudes, or character traits that were required for advanced civilization. Today, we recognize that these explanations rest on a number of indefensible claims about biological differences, innate abilities, intelligence, and race; we also understand that such explanations have been used as justifications for imperialism and colonialism, and have contributed to the transparently self-congratulatory Eurocentric narrative of world history. But until fairly recently, our condemnation of these colonialist narratives was based primarily on the wrongness of racism and oppression; we did not have, in addition to this justified moral outrage, a readily available counter-narrative with scientific explanatory power. Recent developments in human genetics and molecular biology have allowed historians, anthropologists, and archeologists to show that the main causal factor that explains why some nations became wealthy and powerful, while others did not, is geography.

One of the more influential books in this new wave of research is Jared Diamond's *Guns, Germs, and Steel: the Fates of Human Societies*, which considers New Guinea in great detail. It turns out that a number of geographically determined environmental factors limited what was possible on that island. For example, the environment of New Guinea could not support the cultivation of nutrient-rich cereal grains, nor did it contain large domesticatable animals, which could be used as a high-protein food and also as a source of power for agricultural and other uses. And because of the topographical features of the island, small village-based groups were isolated from each other, and the total sustainable population was limited. When the environment of New Guinea is compared to that of the 'fertile crescent' region of the Near East, or to that of the middle region of Eurasia, it becomes clear that some geographical regions have had all the essential resources to support the rapid growth of civilization, while others have not. And when other cases from around the globe are considered, the basic geographical hypothesis is repeatedly confirmed.

Hegel's philosophy of history is often taken to represent the ultimate arrogance of the Eurocentric narrative, and to be connected somehow with the nineteenth- and twentieth-century justifications of imperialism and colonization. Indeed, many have argued that Hegel's supposed 'end of history' thesis amounts to ideological self-congratulation, and that his dismissal of non-European states is blatantly racist. But it is difficult to reconcile these all too common criticisms with what Hegel actually said, and the recent research that investigates the influence of geography on the fates of the world's peoples adds a touch of irony to this misunderstanding.

In the Introduction to Hegel's *Lectures on the Philosophy of History*, one finds a very long section titled, 'Geographical Basis of History,' in which Hegel makes a number of arguments that would fit perfectly well in the pages of Diamond's *Guns, Germs, and Steel*. Hegel did not have access to any research in human genetics and molecular biology, of course, but among the many geographical and environmental factors he considers important in steering the course of world history, are gunpowder, iron and steel, and the environmental prerequisites for domesticating large animals (LPH 114; PH 82). When Hegel considers the relationship between basic environmental factors and the development of civilization, he observes that 'in the Frigid and in the Torrid zone the locality of World-historical peoples cannot be found' (PH 80). Hegel's explanation for this is based on the physiological requirements for survival, and the extent to which a particular environment makes it more or less difficult to satisfy these requirements; in his view, none of basic factors that shaped world history have anything to do with race or human biological differences. It is unfortunate that Hegel's philosophy has been wrongly associated with the discredited racist and colonialist narrative of history, but it is positively shocking to realize that he was actually making the argument that today animates the leading anti-racist and anti-colonialist explanation that now enjoys growing scientific support.

These misunderstandings can be avoided, of course, if one simply goes to the source and reads Hegel's text; and happily, this is easy to do in this case, because his *Philosophy of History* is typically considered to be more accessible than any of his other writings. This was due in large part to Hegel's desire to reach a wider audience in the 1820s through his recurring public lectures on the philosophy of history (delivered every other year in Berlin, from 1822 to 1831); these lectures were fast solidifying his status as the most prominent philosopher in Germany, and he accordingly devoted a great deal of energy to them. In addition to the *Philosophy of History*, though, we must also consider his comments on history in the *Philosophy of Right*, especially since Hegel himself suggested to his students that it could almost serve as textbook for his course (PH 1/LPH 11). In this chapter, then, I will consider: (i) the idea that 'reason rules the world,' which rests on the distinction between necessity and contingency in history, (ii) the overall path of freedom, (iii) progressivism and the 'end of history,' and (iv) the twilight of the modern state.

i. NECESSITY AND CONTINGENCY IN HISTORY

Hegel's basic claim at the beginning of the *Introduction* is that 'reason governs the world,' that history is a 'rational process' (LPH 27/ PH 9), and this is consistent with his claim that some sort of necessity is at work in other domains from nature to consciousness, and so on. This may already sound like a sufficiently controversial claim, but when Hegel adds references to the 'cunning of reason' (PH 33), as though reason were some sort of 'thing' or 'agent' with its own goals and dispositions, his view seems to move from controversial to recklessly implausible. And Hegel also claims that the goal of history is 'the consciousness of freedom' (LPH 53–4), that the rational process of history is somehow aiming to produce collections of individuals who come to have full awareness and understanding of their own basic principle, that is, freedom. So, in accordance with Hegel's thinking about the deep reciprocal link between freedom and reason, reason captures both the essence of history and its goal.

But of course, Hegel was not the first philosopher to approach human history in this manner. In his *Idea for a Universal History* (1784), Kant argues that human history will yield an overall pattern and purpose: behind the actual intentions of individuals, and beneath all of the idiocy and chaos of human affairs, there might be found nature's hidden plan to evoke our highest rational capacities. Ironically, Kant suggests, it is because of our 'unsocial sociability,' our deep need to live in societies that nonetheless force our interests and desires to clash with those of others, that we can develop our capacity for organization, compromise, law, and an understanding of justice (KS 418). The highest expression of freedom will come about, Kant argues, only when societies full of debate and dispute about its exact nature are forced to set its meaning in law, in a constitution. And, he adds, we must accept that progress towards this end will involve suffering, war, revolution, setbacks, and exhaustion (KS 420). Kant argues that although nature's hidden plan is often difficult to discern, it is nonetheless an appropriate object of study for philosophers, and if philosophers can succeed in articulating nature's plan, they may even be able to accelerate the rate at which humanity approaches its goal.

But for Kant, no perfect or complete solution for humanity will ever be found, because our flawed nature ultimately prevents it: 'from such crooked wood as man is made of, nothing perfectly straight can be built' (KS 419). Nor is nature's plan even something we can have true knowledge of, that is, it cannot be a finding of reason or subject to any sort of proof. Still, though, he urges that we must nonetheless postulate its truth (just as we make a number of other postulates in his view), as a kind of rationally justified faith, because it is a condition for the possibility of reconciling ourselves to the world.

Kant's philosophy of history clearly frames the questions that Hegel (along with others at the end of the eighteenth century) starts with. Kant calls the necessary structure of history that underlies all of its contingencies the 'secret plan of nature'; Hegel adopts the same idea and calls it 'cunning of reason.' Both philosophers, then, claim that behind all of the historical events that may seem random, accidental, or chaotic, and beneath the unpredictable competition of human interests and passions, there is nonetheless something else going on, a deeper narrative with a different sort of explanatory power. Both Kant and Hegel are making a distinction between history in the familiar sense of observable events, influences, and causes (historical events), and history in the philosophical sense, as the process that retrospectively illuminates how we have collectively become who we are (historical narrative). These two types of history may also be said to capture different sorts of necessity, 'external' and 'internal' respectively, where the former signifies the sort of causal necessity that binds the physical world, and the latter signifies the way the philosophical narrative is bound by the development of its own conceptual structure. But in the same way that he modified Kant's view of teleology in living organisms, by arguing for a stronger claim than mere postulation, Hegel here argues that the necessary structure of history is part of the general structure of the world, which is something that we can, in fact, understand and know.

In the 1822 and 1828 versions of *Introduction*, Hegel distinguishes between 'original,' 'reflective,' and 'philosophical' history (PH 1–8/LPH 11–24). On this taxonomy, the practice of 'original' history requires that both historian and the object of study share the same set of cultural, linguistic, and political influences; this does not mean that an original historian cannot be critical or poetic, but rather that any critical or poetic element present in this sort of history will be situated in the same way as the events relayed. 'Reflective' history, then, will involve some disparity between the situatedness of the historian and the situatedness of the history at issue, whether because the study traverses a variety of historical periods, because it attempts to translate an earlier period into the terms of the present one, or because it stands outside of and interrogates the situated self-understanding of an historical period. Philosophical (or 'speculative') history, though, according to Hegel, is the enterprise of articulating the basic organizing principles of human history taken as a whole, showing that there is reason or structure to what happens that ties everything together and explains the reality that we all find ourselves in at present. This method of history, practiced by both Kant and Hegel, requires that one sort out which of the known or observable events in history are part of the underlying philosophical narrative, and which can be set aside as mere accidents. And again, it must be remembered that neither Kant nor Hegel expects to find people in history who are fully aware of this philosophical narrative (PH 25).

This distinction between necessity and contingency is complex, especially in the context of formal logic; but Hegel does not think about the distinction in terms of formal logic, and he often avails himself of it in perfectly ordinary and intuitive ways. He suggests in the *Encyclopedia* that when we are engaged in careful consideration of the world, we are already implicitly making a distinction between which features of the world are insignificant and could just as well be otherwise, and which features seem more essential or fundamental (ENCI § 6). In general, if something is contingent, then it could either occur or not; but then, its happening or not happening will necessarily determine other events. For example, whether or not a person is allergic to bee stings is a contingency, and whether or not some bee will sting me is a contingency as well; but if it turns out that I am allergic, and it also turns out that some bee stings me, then my allergic reaction will follow by necessity. So in cases like this one, contingency determines necessity. But this example is a bit too narrow for Hegel's real agenda, because the sort of necessity it points out is causal necessity, and Hegel often thinks of causal necessity as a kind of 'external' necessity, because it does not capture the 'internal' necessity he sees in the development of the *a priori* philosophical narrative of history.

Examples that better illustrate his use of the distinction between necessity and contingency are the fates of both ordinary and exceptional people in history, as well as the fortunes of whole peoples and states. Hegel thinks that the fortunes of ordinary people are paradigmatic cases of contingency: any person might contract a terminal illness, suffer the experience of random violence, meet a person who changes everything, or win the lottery. These are all things that could just as well occur or not. But Hegel thinks the same way about exceptional people too, as when he considers the role of passion in history, or the effects of 'world-historical individuals.' When he claims that 'nothing great happens without individual passion,' Hegel just means to point out that when actual people are involved in historical events, they are typically motivated by their narrow self-interest and passions; but the necessity here is just that someone or other be motivated enough to act, not that any specific person be moved by passion (PH 23–4). Likewise, Hegel's comments about 'world-historical individuals,' that is, those figures in history who seem to make big things happen, show that in each case, if it had not been that person to make history, there would have been someone else to show up and do the same thing (PH 29–31). The overall stages of development in history have a necessary structure and sequence, according to Hegel, but the specifiable players involved in these events are contingent. And on a more general level, there are cases throughout history of whole societies being wiped out by one contingency or another, from plagues and natural disasters to eradication by the forces of hostile invaders; empirical history, Hegel says, will often seem like 'the slaughter-bench at which the happiness of peoples, the wisdom of states, and virtue of individuals have been victimized' (PH 21).

But constructing the kind of philosophical narrative that Hegel is after will have to avoid the tendency to read into history exactly what one wants to find, to impose an *a priori* scheme on the facts. If one falls prey to this liability, one might simply ignore any facts that do not fit the story, and make much of those that confirm it. This is why Hegel is at pains to insist (in a seemingly paradoxical fashion) that a philosophical history must proceed in a rigorously empirical fashion: not a facile empiricism that refuses to make any distinctions at all between what is important and unimportant in history, disingenuously claiming to be free of bringing any theoretical constructions whatever to bear on historical data (this would anyway be impossible), but an empiricism that is attentive to all the facts and responsible for the *a priori* principles it employs.

Hegel's philosophical narrative of history presupposes that its structure is at least as accessible to us as the structure of natural history. In the case of natural history, most people are quite willing to accept that there is a kind of 'reason,' or 'structure,' or necessity going on, even when observing a complex natural object that has no immediately discernable order or structure. Anyone who looks at, say, a pond ecosystem, and is baffled at the question whether any organizing principles could be specified, would nonetheless assume that an ecologist could arrive on the scene and show that events in the pond are 'governed by reason.' The ecologist could explain how events occur in accordance with various chemical, biological, and mechanical systems, and also in ways compatible with natural selection; a philosophically minded ecologist could even introduce some ways of grasping the complex organic whole as it changes and develops over time. But for many people, everything changes when we move from natural to human history; once individual human beings are involved, they say, there is no reason, structure, or laws that govern what occurs, because human beings are fundamentally non-natural, and possess free wills that obey no form of necessity. So, the objection might continue, any *a priori* scheme one claims to find at work behind human history will be a wishful and self-serving fabrication.

Hegel does think that when 'sprit' emerges from nature, it represents a qualitative break, but not one that rules out reason in history. Hegel does not think that human beings are metaphysically distinct from nature, and he rejects the notion that our thinking and freedom obey a separate set of rules than those governing nature. 'Spirit' emerges from nature whenever human beings start to reflect on their desires and interests, which amounts to a self-distancing process that tends to lead to complex, rule-governed, language-using human groups. If the contingent features of empirical history allow for it, these human groups will develop some reflexive awareness of themselves, and some understanding of shared interests and values. This reflexive awareness leads human groups to become self-organizing and self-legislating, which does represent a distancing from the structure of nature, but Hegel thinks that we can nonetheless discern the structure of thought and consciousness, and that some features of this structure will be recapitulated versions of what we found in nature. 'Spirit' supervenes on nature and gradually forges its own narrative history, which will turn out to be the story of coming to know itself, struggling towards a point where its self-understanding will be adequate to its essential nature (PH 18, 72).

ii. THE PATH OF FREEDOM

When Hegel surveys world history, the basic story that emerges is the movement from societies in which 'one is free,' to societies where 'some are free,' and finally to societies in which 'all are free' (PH 19, 54–79); alternatively, one could say that the progression is from dictatorship to oligarchy to democracy. As he sees it, these stages are represented by 'the Orient,' the Greeks, and Germanic nations (which includes all of Northern Europe, Scandinavia, and Britain), and so it is in the last stage that we find the modern state, which allows for the full expression of 'subjective,' 'objective,' and 'absolute' freedom. In accordance with his speculative hermeneutics, Hegel argues that the goal of history, the full realization of freedom, is internally generated from human history itself, from the various human struggles and strivings over time. And he takes this position to be consistent with his general philosophical approach, in which he rejects 'givens,' whether this is a reference to some metaphysical feature of the world, an intuition, or a supernatural deity's will (PHG § 76). It is because we reject all of these traditional 'givens,' and because we do not try to invent or seek to discover foundational principles to be applied to history, that we are left with history itself as the final appeal, the 'last court of judgment' (PR §§ 341–5; LHP1 1–7, 50–5).

The idea of freedom, according to Hegel, took a certain shape in ancient Greek society and a different one in Roman society: freedom in the latter case had, for example, internalized a much stronger sense of individual rights based on property, and so the Romans, he argues, understood freedom largely in these terms. It is not that the timeless idea of freedom includes such individualist features and that only the Romans were able to apprehend them; rather, the historical conditions were conducive to the Romans developing a conception of freedom that seemed to them to resolve some of the tensions between individual and state that existed in Greek society (PHG §§ 464–83). Whereas the primary issue for ancient interpretations of freedom, and for the supersession of Greek society by Roman society, was property rights, the development from the ancient world to the modern world is characterized by the reinterpretation of these individual rights in light of the rise of Christianity and the French Revolution (PR § 124). In all cases, the idea of freedom is something that can only be articulated in terms of a specific historical period and culture, and is also something that must be conceived as part of a developing process. Whatever we think about freedom today will draw on this historical development and be mediated by our particular culture. We have our current conception of freedom because we stand on the shoulders of previous societies that have tried to realize their own visions of freedom, and not because we have special access to the truth. But even if we accept that the origin of the idea of freedom is historical, and that it has shaped the guiding aspirations of modernity, one might still object that freedom is functioning in Hegel's philosophy as a foundation, as a supposedly Archimedean point from which he develops his theory; but, one might say, this is precisely the sort of 'given' that Hegel took himself to avoid. The objection might continue that there are other ideas that have either come on the scene or developed in history, say, virtue, power, or justice, and that there is no non-arbitrary way of claiming that one of these values is more fundamental than the others. In response to this, Hegel argues that history actually turned out to favor freedom as the fundamental value, and that this makes sense given other features of modernity: given the 'death of God' that characterizes the modern period, we are left with a kind of groundlessness, and can choose either nihilism or the project of figuring out how to be self-grounding and genuinely free (LHP 47–9). So it is not that freedom is inherently interesting, or that it was supported by the strongest arguments; it is rather just that history turned out to favor this question of freedom above all others.

The *Philosophy of Right* seems to begin with the idea of freedom as a kind of foundational principle, a 'given' from which the entire structure of the modern state is derived. But even there, the starting point of the argument is actually an interpretation, specifically the interpretation of freedom that, in Hegel's view, captures our particularly modern way of thinking. He does think that the modern state better actualizes freedom than any previous state in history, but he does not start the *Philosophy of Right* with that historical argument: instead of trying to show that the modern state resolves tensions that plagued earlier states, he starts with the modern state as it exists and attempts to draw out of it what is rational, its most defensible features, its systematic strengths, and its capacity (at its best) to satisfy our modern understanding of freedom (PR 21).

It is also significant, though, that Hegel works out his conception of freedom in the context of political philosophy: freedom depends on the existence of the state, and the various conceptions of freedom in history have always been correlated with particular states. The philosophical reasons for this correlation are that people can only become maximally free in the context of a state that supports all of the essential aspects of 'ethical life,' that states have the rule of law and constitutions, which lend objectivity to our conception of freedom, and that states support art, religion, and philosophy, the forms of 'absolute spirit' (PH 38–9, 43–5, 49–50). States attempt to satisfy the criteria they set out for themselves, and here again, the language of organisms and nature shapes Hegel's account: states are organisms, which go through typical stages of growth, striving, satisfaction, decay, and death (LPH 58–60). Other reasons for this correlation are very practical, and have to do with the many state functions that stabilize and secure the structure of 'ethical life.' For example, in ancient civilizations, political organization required record-keeping, and this lead to written languages, documented histories, and lasting accounts of communal self-reflection. States also have the task of making sure that the gains of history are not lost, that there is no retrogression in the narrative that stretches from 'one is free' to 'all are free' (PH 54–79; PR § 356). Hegel insists that, despite whatever contingent factors may be at play, states are the best defense against losing the gains of supersession through history.

Given that states and peoples are the main vehicles for the development of freedom in history, it is worth pointing out that Hegel does not think that these carriers of 'spirit' are coextensive with any ethnicity, race, or religious group that claims to have been 'chosen by God' (PH 58–9). Nor does he think that 'spirit' requires a state or people to be ethnically homogeneous or 'pure' in some superficial sense; in fact, Hegel tends to credit ethnic heterogeneity as a mark of achievement, because it shows that a society is no longer immersed in the natural conditions of its origin. Hegel even argues that it was the influence of foreigners and the resulting heterogeneity that made ancient Greece such a remarkably vibrant and creative place to be (PH 225–7). What matters about a state, for

Hegel, is its conception of freedom and the ways that this conception is expressed in politics, codified in law, structured by institutions, and reflected upon in art, religion, and philosophy.

It is in this context that the New Guinea case is interesting, because it shows that however unfamiliar Hegel's claims may seem to us, we must be careful to avoid drawing the wrong implications from them. Hegel thinks that the path of freedom in history moves across Asia and settles in Europe, and so by extension, fails to take root in any other regions of the world, but his argument for this path is based on principles that have nothing to do with racism, Eurocentrism, or imperialism. In fact, it is in this context that Hegel claims that the path of freedom will, in the future, leave Europe and take up residence in America, mainly because of its distinctive geographical features: because of its vast territory and natural resources, North America will be able to avoid much of the discontent that has characterized the aging and crowded states of Europe. Hegel even suggests, in a comment that seems incompatible with Eurocentrism, that 'America is therefore the land of the future, where in the ages that lie before us, the burden of the World's History shall reveal itself' (PH 86).

iii. PROGRESSIVISM AND THE 'END OF HISTORY'

Hegel's philosophy of history is certainly committed to a kind of progressivism, but only regarding the philosophical *a priori* narrative of history, not regarding empirical history. There is nothing in the philosophical narrative that implies that all historical change is progress, nor likewise that any appeal to the status quo is by itself an argument for anything; if one wants to celebrate some feature of the status quo, one must provide an argument that shows that this feature expresses the best way of thinking about the matter, that it resolves the tensions or difficulties of other views, or that it proves more satisfying than other interpretations (LHP1 49–100). Hegel allows that empirical history can one moment push the envelope of what is possible for philosophical history, but then halt and stagnate, or even regress (PHG §§ 582–98; LHP1 3). Simply pointing out that people believe certain things today, that this or that is 'the way things are done around here' leaves all the interesting and difficult work undone. And given that empirical history often takes a step backwards, preventing this from happening, Hegel thinks, is worthy of struggle and sacrifice. And preventing retrogression requires arguments that reject the simpleminded progressivism that collapses the distinction between philosophical and empirical history.

Hegel's combination of philosophical progressivism and, what we might call, 'empirical realism,' generates arguments about supersession that are attentive to the facts on the ground at the same time. For example, Hegel argues that once the strong notion of the individual with property rights came on the scene in Roman society, no one could go back to the naïve harmony of Greece: the tensions in Greek society represented by their tragedies were resolved in Roman society (PHG §§ 477–83; 464–76). And Hegel was particularly concerned about the Terror that followed the French Revolution, as a case of post-revolution retrogression. And on a more general level of Hegel's system, consider his claim that philosophy is a supersession of religion, because once we see that philosophy articulates the same features of the world that religion does but without mysticism and reference to the arbitrary authority of the supernatural, we can no longer think that religion is an entirely satisfying mode of thought (PHG §§ 207–30; §§ 672–787).

The main point about these kinds of narratives is that retrogression is ironic: there is a sense of philosophical progress, against which going backwards is mystifying and unjustifiable. For example, the Hegelian argument against slavery proceeds not by making reference to ahistorical or preternatural human rights, but by arguing that there is an historical story to be told about a time when people did not have the conceptual maturity to condemn slavery, but that eventually the idea came on the scene that all people should be treated equally with respect and rights (perhaps with the arrival of the 'soul hypothesis' of Christianity), that it became intelligible to condemn slavery on those grounds, and that this gave rise to a richer and more satisfying interpretation of what it is to be human than ever before; this became something that, in the sense described above, we cannot go back on. The same sort of argument might be made about universal suffrage, civil rights, and perhaps even some

contemporary shifts in thinking about environmentalism and eco-
logical sustainability; but again, the point is that any of these cases
stand in need of an argument that shows them to be genuine
supersessions, and that argument will need to be couched in terms
of the distinction between philosophical and empirical history. And
whenever we have identified a genuine supersession, we treat it as
something that we cannot go back on, which, in Hegel's language,
means that these gains are 'absolute' and that they have 'stepped
out of history.'

If Hegel's view is that empirical history is not automatically pro-
gressive, and that, even when the philosophical narrative of history
takes a step forward, retrogressions are always empirically possible,
what are we to make of his claims in the *Lectures on the Philosophy
of History* that seem to suggest that we have reached the 'end of
history'? First of all, the same point just made about progressivism
applies here as well: whatever Hegel means by the 'end' of history, it
should be applied only to philosophical history, not empirical history. Obviously, empirical history does not come to an end, and
Hegel does not at all need to deny this. He does refer to 'our own
time' as the 'last stage in history,' and this claim has at least one
clear and intuitive meaning: in the overall path of freedom from
'one is free' to 'some are free' to 'all are free,' if we correctly take
ourselves and our modern world to have acquired the philosophical
realization that 'all are free,' then it is not clear where else we can go.
There may of course be lots of work to be done in fully actualizing
the idea that 'all are free,' including the reform of public policy
and law, but the basic notion that 'all are free' seems hard to
improve on.

But then again, pointing out that our current understanding of
freedom seems hard to improve is not the same thing as making an
argument that any such improvement is impossible. But if we say
that philosophical history has come to an end, we must mean that
we somehow know that there are no further supersessions to be
had, that improvement is impossible. Phrasing the 'end of history'
thesis as a claim about the future, which it surely must be, makes it
clear, though, why Hegel cannot endorse it. Recall that Hegel's
speculative hermeneutics is limited to retrospective interpretation:

in the Preface to the *Philosophy of Right*, he argues that everyone is a 'child of his time' and that philosophy is 'its own time comprehended in thought' (PR 22). Hegel consistently rejects utopian criticism, because its force is generated from claims about possible future states of affairs, and he argues that it is not philosophy's job to 'issue instructions' about how the world ought to be in the future (PR 22–3). His view is that philosophy, because it is essentially backward-looking and affirmative towards the rationality of the present, has nothing to say about the future; and when philosophy seems to have a lot to say about the present, we can deduce that the present state of affairs is already in decline. 'When philosophy paints its grey in grey,' Hegel says, 'a shape of life has grown old, and it cannot be rejuvenated, but only recognized, by the grey in grey of philosophy; the owl of Minerva begins its flight only with the onset of dusk' (PR 23). Philosophy can retrospectively discern whether our current stage in history is mature, but in such cases, it cannot say anything about what is on the horizon; but claiming that we have reached the end of philosophical history is also claiming something about the future, namely, that it will contain no further stages of the philosophical narrative.

Unless we assume that, while writing about the philosophy of history, Hegel abandoned his deepest convictions about the nature of philosophy, we must consider that the 'end of history' really means the 'consummation' of history. If we take this to be Hegel's meaning, then the idea of the 'end of history' suddenly seems entirely consistent with his overall view: philosophy looks backwards and reconstructs the development of freedom up to the present, which will then appear as the consummation of the whole process. And this may anyway be a permanent feature of the present, that it always seems to us to be the consummation of past development. Experiencing the present as the consummation of the past, though, generates no confidence that our current stage of development will not itself be superseded, since there may yet be new tensions that turn out to be irresolvable. Or we might discover later that our apparent supersession of a previous stage was based on a misunderstanding, or that the criteria for satisfaction were misapprehended, and so on. There must always be a sense of provisionality and fallibility that accompanies our current self-understanding; indeed, Hegel argues that our ability to have such doubts about our current self-understanding is itself the historical accomplishment of the Enlightenment (PHG § 19; PH 55). The practice of self-doubt and self-criticism itself is a feature of modern life that counts as a supersession of pre-modern dogmatism.

With these points in mind, we should be wary of any temptation to be smug about our current place in history. We may see it as the consummation of the path of freedom, and we may have no idea what may come next, but so long as we take ourselves to be practicing Hegelian philosophy, we must adopt some humility about ourselves and our assessment of the current state of affairs. We should not worry, then, that a Hegelian state would produce a population of Nietzsche's 'last men,' that is, those who have become sluggishly content and smugly self-satisfied with the world, and for whom there are no remaining ideals to arouse the passions. And we should also avoid thinking that there is nothing left to do in the modern state but work towards piecemeal reform, on the thought that nothing radical can happen after the 'end of history.'

iv. THE TWILIGHT OF THE MODERN STATE

In the *Philosophy of Right*, Hegel takes himself to have articulated the structure of the modern state considered as an 'inherently rational entity'; but if philosophy has been able to see this structure clearly, then it would seem to be 'a shape of life' that has 'grown old' and 'cannot be rejuvenated' (PR 23). This is the critical dimension of Hegel's speculative hermeneutics: portraying the rationality of a thing may sometimes save it from external criticisms based on merely contingent features, but it may also show that the rationality of that thing is unstable, incomplete, or doomed to collapse. Hegel seems to be saying that the modern state is in its twilight and that it will soon be superseded, but if so, what are the tensions or contradictions of the modern state that are irresolvable?

Hegel thinks that the capitalist free market is an essential feature of the modern state, but one that carries with it a number of problems. We need the free market, he says, because it institutionalizes an important kind of freedom for individuals, namely the freedom to enter into private contracts and relations of exchange, where goods, property, and services become the fungible media of pure recognition. But at the same time, he knows that there are many problems associated with capitalism, including poverty, periodic market failure, monopoly, imperialism, and the concentration of power in the hands of the very wealthy. Many of these problems are caused by contingencies, Hegel thinks, and so do not necessarily present any difficulty for the portrayal of the state as 'inherently rational.' So, for example, we can assume that there will be a contingent distribution of skills and aptitudes in any population, and that this will tend to produce an inequality of life outcomes in a competitive market economy (PR § 200). We can also assume that the interests of producers and consumers will never be perfectly matched, and that even if the market has self-correcting mechanisms, there will nonetheless always be some whose interests are thwarted (PR § 236).

But some problems of the free market seem to be more than mere contingencies, and present a different kind of challenge for the claim that the modern state is rational, stable, and capable of satisfying the criteria we have established for it. For example, Hegel acknowledges that capitalism requires constant growth, which drives it towards overproduction and the quest for new markets through imperialism; he even describes these tendencies as the 'inner dialectic of society' (PR §§ 245–8). He also knows that a free market economy tends to distribute wealth unequally, which produces both a class of people tied to overspecialized labor and thrust towards poverty, as well as a class of people with excessive wealth and power (PR §§ 243–5). The main problem with poverty, for Hegel, is that it effectively removes people from 'ethical life' and therefore denies them the status of person and citizen; poverty interferes with the institutional structure of freedom, which then excludes people from education, health care, and equal treatment under the law (PR § 241). And as poverty becomes more pervasive and entrenched, it provides the grounds for the development of a 'rabble mentality': individuals who are impoverished have lost 'that feeling of right, integrity, and honor which comes from supporting oneself by one's own activity and work' (PR § 244). Revealingly, Hegel also thinks that the wealthy can develop a 'rabble mentality' as well: from the moment they start to think they can buy anyone or anything they wish, they have effectively cut themselves off from 'ethical life' (PR § 246ft). The capitalist free market tends to produce the extremes of poverty and wealth, Hegel argues, along with the 'physical and ethical corruption common to both' (PR § 185).

Some of the problems associated with the free market, though, can be addressed by state regulation and intervention, as well as by certain institutions of civil society. For example, Hegel imagines that government agencies can regulate the market to some extent, and can also help those who suffer the vagaries of the market through no fault of their own (PR § 236). One such agency, which Hegel calls the 'police' (*Polizei*), will control the pricing of any commodities considered to be necessities; in the case of, say, a bad annual crop, the 'police' will enact temporary price-fixing to ensure that essentials remain affordable. And the 'corporations' (*Korporationen*) involved with certain trades and professions will help as well, since they look after the welfare of their members, especially regarding the conditions of work and trades, but also generally in their function as a 'second family.'

Hegel's treatment of poverty and other market failures in the *Philosophy of Right* begins by characterizing them as mere contingencies with adequate remedies, but as he explores these remedial options, he seems to settle on the view that these are systemic issues that may not be so easily managed. Hegel suggests charity in passing as yet another partial solution, but then admits that there are no genuinely lasting answers here. Ultimately, he seems to throw up his hands in saying that 'the important question of how poverty can be remedied is one which agitates and torments modern societies especially' (PR § 244). But this creates a problem for Hegel's view, because it shifts the burden to the state, which places the general good above the interests of the market, and is increasingly empowered to interfere with civil society as poverty increases (PR § 236A, 185A); but the more the state intervenes, on his view, the less civil society can be regarded as domain of freedom for individuals and 'corporations.' Hegel needs civil society to provide individual freedoms, the socialization of needs as individuals integrate themselves into the whole 'system of needs,' and the legal recognition of individual rights in a public system of justice. He also needs the institutionalization of *Bildung* in the context of the 'corporations' so that citizens can be educated and acculturated to identify with 'ethical life' and develop into full citizens who are prepared to participate in the collective self-reflection of the state.

The account of the state in the *Philosophy of Right*, then, contains a precarious balance between civil society and the state. Hegel presents a number of systemic tendencies of the free market that threaten the stability of 'ethical life,' but which can only be remedied sufficiently by increased state power, which itself also threatens the balance of 'ethical life.' It may be that this uneasy compromise just is the nature of the modern state, and that there is no more satisfying resolution to be found; but it is not likely that Hegel would accept this. Some Hegel scholars, though, have argued that his conception of the 'corporation' is rich with implications that, if followed through, would suggest a different sort of political arrangement than Hegel envisioned. Indeed, even in the years just after Hegel's death, his student and colleague, Edward Gans (who compiled the additions in the *Philosophy of Right*), accepted the idea that civil society would produce great inequality and poverty, and sought to expand the scope of corporate power such that 'corporations' would function much like contemporary trade unions, which would solve the problems of civil society by establishing something like syndicalism, where unions are effectively more powerful than the state.

This is an interesting interpretation of the *Philosophy of Right*, because it takes seriously the critical implications of the Preface, where Hegel comments on the role of philosophy and the signs of when a 'shape of life' has 'grown old.' But this interpretation also tries to remain true to Hegel's speculative hermeneutics, which seeks the 'rational in the real': the 'corporations' already exist in some form or other, and may contain the germ of a genuine resolution to the tensions and contradictions of the modern capitalist state. Hegel seems open to such a possibility since a labor union would be perfect example of a *Korporation*: they are typically defined by a specific trade, and ideally have a clear link to a politics of the common good. But, of course, the labor union is not the only plausible example; non-profit organizations, political action committees, and such, are also good candidates for voluntary associations that might satisfy Hegel's criteria (PR 270R, 288). In any case, the important thing is that the *Korporationen* are not allowed to do anything that is opposed to general public welfare, though, he admits, the limits of state intervention to ensure this will always be debatable and subject to continued interpretation (PR § 234).

It is even possible that Hegel would have to reject the notion that a business corporation could count as a *Korporation*. In both the *Philosophy of Right* and the *Phenomenology*, Hegel has the suspicion that wealth and profit interests will undermine any conception of the common good. The business corporation, in its contemporary form is by definition not an organization that can aim to integrate its activities with the common good; rather, it is designed to further the interests of its stockholders, and cannot act on the sort of general considerations the Hegel thinks must be in play. Hegel acknowledges that business corporations are beneficial to society and play an important economic role, but he could not grant them the status of a 'corporation' (PR § 254). If business corporations were excluded from the negotiations of the *Korporationen*, then the overall political arrangement would be syndicalism of some variety; but then, this may be tantamount to the withering away of the state, which would be just as unacceptable as the withering away of civil society: on the account in the *Philosophy of Right*, 'ethical life' must have a functional harmony between civil society and a state.

In any case, this instability between civil society and the state, as a result of the 'inner dialectic' of the capitalist free market, marks a fundamental ambiguity of Hegel's *Philosophy of Right*. We are left with open questions about how to evaluate the necessary and contingent features of our modern state, and even with the question whether our modern state is the same as Hegel's, or whether we have already experienced some supersessions that separate us from him. We might also wonder whether we are facing new contingencies, unanticipated by Hegel, that threaten to destroy the gains of modern state and interfere with the path of freedom in history. One example of this sort of contingency is the contemporary environmental crisis, including global warming, widespread contamination of air and water, overpopulation, and the unsustainable overuse of natural resources, fossil fuels, and such. Many environmentalists argue that environmental sustainability is incompatible with the modern state, and that the reform necessary for sustainability might well drastically change the nature of the state; in Hegel's terms, the problem is that the environmental crisis might force the modern state as we know to be superseded. There is nothing in Hegel's philosophy of history that could justify our dismissing this possibility, and nothing in his political philosophy that rules it out either. But even if we suppose that the contemporary Western liberal democratic version of the state is the model that best captures Hegelian freedom, and that there are no potentially destructive contingencies to worry about, there is nonetheless much still to be done to fully actualize freedom.

CHAPTER 7

ABSOLUTE SPIRIT: ART, RELIGION, AND PHILOSOPHY

A philosophizing *without system* cannot be scientific at all . . . A content has its justification only as a moment of the whole, outside of which it is only an unfounded presupposition or a subjective certainty. Many philosophical writings restrict themselves like this – to the mere utterance of *dispositions* and *opinions*. It is erroneous to understand by 'system' a philosophy whose principle is restricted and [kept] distinct from other principles; on the contrary, it is the principle of genuine philosophy to contain all particular principles within itself. (ENCI § 14)

Each of the previous chapters begins with an example or case study, which then functions as an entry-point into some part of Hegel's philosophy: foxes, hedgehogs, and the basic dispositions of philosophers (Chapter 1), enhancement technologies and alienation as modern malaises (Chapter 2), Dostoyevsky's novel about a man with a self-defeating conception of freedom (Chapter 3), convergent evolution and the deep structure of nature (Chapter 4), Ornette Coleman's higher-order reflection on jazz (Chapter 5), and the influence of geography on New Guinea's development through history (Chapter 6); but is there anything that connects all of these disparate cases, anything they all have in common? If one identifies with the 'tough-minded' fox, then these cases might appear to be a random collection, and any attempt to bring them together will seem artificial. But even with sympathies for the 'tender-minded' hedgehog, one may struggle to figure out how these disparate cases can be brought together and seen as a unity.

In response to this sort of question, Hegel would turn the table. He would argue that since the world is, and has always been, a complex structured whole and an organic unity, the challenge is not how to find or fabricate a unity, but how to recover and reconstruct the unity that has been eclipsed. He suspects that most of the history of philosophy has been a series of attempts to break up and subdivide the whole, and that this has effectively colonized our habits of thinking and weakened our ability to see the whole in addition to the parts; but 'systematic' philosophy invites us to seek a level of complexity and dynamism in our thought that can match that of the whole. Hegel's argument here is straightforward: if the world is a structured dynamic whole, with some set of basic organizing principles, and we are the part of that whole that has come to develop thinking, and even the sort of thinking that comes to understand the entire system that gave rise to it, then there is no reason in principle why we could not develop our thinking to the level of sophistication that perfectly overlays the actual structure of the whole. At some point, then, we would expect that the structure of thinking and the structure of reality would converge. In fact, Hegel's view is that there is really just one system of philosophy, not many, and that this one system will include all other sciences, as a 'circle of circles'; and this metaphor suggests that there is no one specific starting point in philosophy, that one can simply jump into the 'system' wherever one likes (ENCI §§ 15–17).

Hegel also thinks that philosophy should be a 'science,' but this is a misleading translation of the German word *Wissenschaft*, because when we think of 'science' we tend to imagine the natural sciences specifically, the so-called 'hard sciences' of physics, chemistry, and biology; but if we have this narrow conception of 'science' in mind, we will misunderstand what Hegel is talking about. *Wissenschaft* has a much broader meaning and can refer to any organized and coherent body of knowledge; this generality is apparent if we consider the other variations: *Naturwissenschaft* (the natural sciences) and *Geisteswissenschaft* (the human sciences).

So, all of the seemingly disparate cases from the previous chapters are actually parts of the same whole; but if we can do no more than point that out, we are not living up to the ambitions of 'systematic' and 'scientific' philosophy. Hegel would be interested in the structural connections and shared organizing principles of these cases, which would pull him into the domains of psychology, psychiatry, art, evolutionary biology, political science, history, anthropology, geography, and of course, philosophy. And the sort of reflection that goes on at this level, Hegel says, since it will continually pull away from contingency, particularity, and idiosyncrasy, will put us in a position to think clearly about our most general values, interests, and aspirations. Hegel calls this type of reflection 'absolute spirit,' and argues that its basic forms are art, religion, and philosophy.

Hegel's only published comments on 'absolute spirit' are in the *Encyclopedia*, and they are brief; but throughout the 1820s his lectures on art, religion, history, and philosophy drew large audiences. Hegel did not publish these lectures in his lifetime, but they were made available after his death, through the work of his students and supporters; the published versions are *Aesthetics: Lectures on Fine Art*, the *Lectures on the History of Philosophy*, and the *Lectures on the Philosophy of Religion*. This chapter considers these forms of 'absolute spirit'; after (i) some general comments on 'absolute' reflection, I will turn to his arguments about (ii) art, (iii) religion, and (iv) philosophy.

i. ABSOLUTELY FUNDAMENTAL VALUES

In the third part of the *Encyclopedia*, the *Philosophy of Mind*, Hegel argues that 'absolute spirit' represents the highest form of reflection for 'spirit,' and takes the forms of art, religion, and philosophy. These forms of 'absolute spirit' share the same object, namely, the basic structure of reality conceived as a dynamic, organic whole (referred to as 'the truth' or 'the absolute'); but they each grasp this structure in different ways, and so represent different forms of knowing: art shows us something about the ultimate structure of reality through sensuous objects, religion represents the same thing symbolically and metaphorically, and philosophy reconstructs the basic structure of reality in the form of pure concepts (ENCIII §§ 553–77). It is through the forms of 'absolute spirit,' Hegel argues, that 'spirit' will ultimately come to know itself.

It is helpful to consider from the outset how 'absolute spirit' relates to other forms of 'the absolute,' and also how it supersedes the 'subjective' and the 'objective' in all of their related domains. If 'absolute spirit' designates the general modes of reflection on our fundamental values and interests, then 'absolute rationality' refers to the general structure of this reflection, and 'absolute freedom' is experienced when one can identify with one's actions and ends as they are mediated by this structure. The structure in question here, that 'absolute spirit' reflects on is broader and more general than the normative structure of any particular group, institution, or state, and is ultimately the most basic structure of reality, whatever that turns out to be.

It is not entirely clear what Hegel thought about the relationship between his conception of 'absolute spirit' in his later works and his notion of 'absolute knowledge' from the *Phenomenology*; but it is plausible, at least, to think that 'absolute knowledge,' which appears in his first attempt to lay out his 'system,' is simply elaborated and expanded to become the 'absolute' forms of 'spirit,' rationality, and freedom in his later, more mature system. In the *Phenomenology*, 'absolute knowledge' is the practice of self-reflective sacrifice and surrender, a way of living in accordance with the results of the entire sequence of internally driven supersessions that make up the narrative of that early work. 'Absolute knowing' is a strategy of 'losing oneself to find oneself': one strives to lose oneself in the matter at hand, to overcome the typically insecure clinging that pulls one towards either the object or one's self, and to grasp the full dissolution of the subject-object distinction (PHG §§ 3, 29, 50, 53, 804–5).

The type of reflection characteristic of 'absolute spirit' will appear to be merely theoretical, or at least detached from any practical or political concerns; this is partially true, but the related ideas of 'absolute rationality' and 'absolute freedom' bring the communal self-reflection of art, religion, and philosophy down to earth and into the context of human affairs. So, for example, on Hegel's view, one becomes maximally free when one acts in accordance with reason at the subjective, objective, and 'absolute' levels, where subjective rationality refers to the practice of formulating and acting on reasons that are intelligible from the individual's point of view, and objective rationality refers to the practices that are organized by the rule-governed structure of institutions, culture, and the state. 'Absolute' rationality, then, requires that one scrutinize the domains of subjective and objective rationality and consider whether their rule-governed structures are coherent, stable, and enduring, and whether they ought to be revised in light of humanity's most fundamental values and interests.

It is worth emphasizing that the practices of 'absolute spirit' are social practices; the type of reflection characteristic of art, religion, and philosophy cannot be fully carried out by a single person. What counts as a good reason, question, or interpretation will be largely determined by the norms of these social practices. There is a kind of circularity at work here that Hegel wants to embrace instead of deny: communal self-reflection must be carried out internally. This higher order reflection must articulate reasons that are public in a broad sense that does not reduce to the kinds of reasons one might call upon when acting according to subjective or objective rationality.

The distinction between the forms of 'absolute spirit,' in Hegel's view, is in part a conceptual distinction that generates what is often called the 'subordination thesis': in terms of their ability to adequately grasp the whole, and to live up to the criteria for knowledge that they set for themselves, art is subordinate to religion, and religion is subordinate to philosophy. Art attempts to grasp the whole through immediate representation, which takes the form of the sensuous and the particular. This is a valid way of expressing the whole, but it tends to be outdone by religion, which introduces concepts and universals that constitute a mediated representation of the whole. Philosophy grasps the world though pure concepts, which Hegel thinks will do the best job of matching the complexity of the whole. But even though Hegel does see the forms of 'absolute spirit' arranged hierarchically, we should not forget that art and religion are still among the highest forms of reflection available to us. And Hegel would add that there are still features of art and religion that philosophy cannot represent conceptually, but which are nonetheless interesting and important. And in any case, 'absolute spirit' in any form is still the 'minded' part of nature coming to know itself through reflection on its most basic values and interests.

Another way of characterizing 'absolute spirit,' which shows both the conceptual unity of its forms as well as their distinctness, is to say that its reflection attempts to undo the work of 'the understanding,' which is perpetually busy with breaking wholes up into parts. Art, religion, and philosophy take the complex, dynamic, and organic whole as their object, and assume that this whole is prior to its parts. Both art and religion, though, will be incapable of getting the part-whole relationship right: art can grasp the whole with some immediacy, but it cannot move towards rigorous comprehension, and although religion can see the parts distinctly, it ultimately fails understand the whole, and so turns to metaphorical thinking and superstition. Only philosophy, Hegel says, can properly understand the parts, the whole, and the part-whole relation. If philosophy is to be 'systematic' and 'scientific,' it cannot rely too heavily on 'the understanding,' and this will distinguish it from much of the work in the social sciences as well.

The forms of 'absolute spirit' can also be distinguished historically, since they each appear and reach their apex at different times in history, though Hegel will use the conceptual distinction as well to explain their historical emergence. In ancient Greece, for example, art grasped the dynamic and organic whole better than any other form of knowledge. Religion, on the other hand, found its stride in the medieval period, and philosophy came into its own in the modern age. In light of Hegel's other writings, we would expect this to be the case, since 'spirit' comes to full awareness in history, at the same time that the conceptual complexity of the world increases. The modern world is a sufficiently complex normative order that only philosophy (including other *wissenschaftlich* disciplines) can match. There were times in history when art and religion better replicated the complexity of the whole, but their times have passed.

There is also a general process though which 'spirit' comes to know itself that mirrors the developmental moments of freedom as self-realization that Hegel explains in the *Philosophy of Right*. Just as the process of becoming free in the modern state has moments of externalization and internalization, so also 'absolute spirit' undergoes these same movements. Art typically involves the externalization of one's will, and the emergence of art in the earliest stages of human civilization moved people to appropriate the external and sensuous stuff of the world for their own purposes. Prior to the emergence of 'spirit,' human beings were immersed in nature, but as art became a form of collective self-reflection, 'spirit' was pulling away from nature. Once 'spirit' stood over and against nature, its appropriation of the sensuous became a kind of externalization of its will. Historically, art is also involved in the internalization of the world back into our conception of selfhood, but here, religion and philosophy tend to capture this dynamic more effectively.

Finally, Hegel's study of 'absolute spirit' is guided by his speculative hermeneutics: for every art, religion, and philosophy he considers, he tries to find the 'rational in the real' and to understand them as practices in a particular historical context. Part of his interpretive approach here requires that he understand the goals and criteria that are internal to the practice; so, for example, Hegel will be particularly interested in what might be called a 'phenomenology of art' whereby he tries to take up the artists' point of view. And just like his speculative hermeneutics in the context of the *Phenomenology*, Hegel will be asking whether the concepts utilized by art, religion, and philosophy are appropriate to their object; if they are not, then these forms of 'absolute spirit' will fail on their own terms.

ii. ART IS A THING OF THE PAST

Art may have many uses, but Hegel is interested in just one, namely, the use of art to express the deepest and most general nature of what is, to capture the unity of the whole. In other words, Hegel's interest in art is particular to the sense in which it has the same object as religion and philosophy. He does not need to deny that art in fact has other uses, whether in the context of politics or personal amusement, but since he thought his account was both descriptively and normatively accurate, he was committed to the position that many, or even most, forms of artistic expression were not really 'art.' And his notion of artistic beauty correlates with this admittedly narrow function of art: an artwork is beautiful to the extent that it expresses the complex dynamic unity of the world (ILA 25–7). More specifically, the beautiful work of art, Hegel says, will express the freedom of 'spirit' at its current stage of historical development; in fact, the freedom that 'spirit' enjoys at any particular time serves as a distillation of the whole dynamic unity that is supposed to be the object of art. In other words, the extent to which 'spirit' has come to know itself, and be 'at home' with itself in the world, is an index of the structured unity of the whole at that moment. When a work of art shows this effectively, there is a convergence between it and 'the absolute'; this is why Hegel considers beauty to be an objective property of art, and not just a way of characterizing the subjective reactions and judgments of people who experience art.

The arts that Hegel is interested in are architecture, sculpture, painting, music, and poetry (ILA 88–95). Each has its own phases of development, moments of perfection, and such, and each has some relation to his three main historical periods of art: 'symbolic,' which captures everything prior to ancient Greece, 'classical,' which roughly centered around Greece in the fifth century BCE, and 'romantic,' which stretches from the late medieval period to the present (ILA 82–7). So, for example, architecture thrived in the symbolic period, sculpture reached a kind of perfection in the classical period, and painting, music, and poetry all flourish in the romantic period. If we imagine the forms of art on a continuum from the most to the least sensuous, we would have a series like this: architecture, sculpture, painting, music, and poetry. Architecture is the most sensuous, but also, Hegel suggests, the least conceptually interesting; as art becomes less sensuous and more abstract, it acquires the ability to express greater degrees of complexity. So, in Hegel's view, sculpture has greater potential to express the whole than architecture, and painting even more so, because its two-dimensional limitation is actually an expressive virtue. Music is distinctive because its expression is mediated by time, which, Hegel suggests, captures the time-bound rhythm of human thinking; but poetry is the form of art that most directly expresses human interiority, because language is the externalization of thought. Hegel thinks that poetry is the least sensuous of the forms of art, and so also the most expressive of complexity.

Hegel's analysis of art follows closely the contours of his philosophy of history: the art of a particular historical period will express the most deeply held values in play, as well as 'spirit's' stage of development at that time, and a series of historical stages will be a series of supersessions. So, for example, Egyptian art and Egyptian religion, as well as Persian and Indian art, are part of the 'symbolic' period; during this time, artists were in an awkward position: as much as they tried to express the whole through their art, the whole itself was so indeterminate that it was not clear what an effective or accurate expression of it would look like. It may sound counterintuitive to say that the whole was 'indeterminate' at some point in history, since it may seem more reasonable to suppose that the world just is what it is, and that its level of determinateness is only a measure of our ability to comprehend it; but for Hegel, our ability to comprehend the world is a fundamental feature of the world itself: the whole at any point in history will be indeterminate or determinate to the extent that 'spirit' has been able to understand it, and feel 'at home' in it. The art of this period, then, was 'symbolic' because it could only point to what it was trying to express; for example, Egyptian art used animal symbols to point towards the whole. But since the whole was, in a way, inexpressible at that time, Hegel questions whether symbolic art can even properly be considered art at all.

Greek or 'classical' art, on the other hand, fared much better in Hegel's view, because it enjoyed the fortuitous convergence of a much more determinate whole made possible by 'spirit's' advances, plus the centrality of beauty among the fundamental values of Greek culture. Sculpture was the artistic medium that brought form and content together perfectly: it did not need to point beyond itself, because its sensuous form fully exhausted its meaning. Greek religion celebrated humanity, as a harmony of body and mind, and their thinking about this harmony and its relation to the whole could be presented sensuously with no remainder. Classical art, then, expressed the overall structure of humanity's deepest concerns and values at that time, and helped people comprehend the whole and feel 'at home' in it.

In Hegel's view, classical art was more effective than any other form of art in history, and represented the first genuine externalization of 'spirit.' But Greek society was changing and soon developed ruptures that could not be resolved with the conceptual resources available to them. At this point, though, Greek drama and poetry, both of which are less sensuous and therefore more capable of expressing complexity than sculpture, would capture these tensions and contradictions. Hegel thought that the best example of Greek drama in its role as the collective self-reflection of 'absolute spirit' was Sophocles' play *Antigone*. He first analyzed *Antigone* in the *Phenomenology of Spirit* to explain the transition from Greek society to Roman society, and he continued to refer to the play in his later writings as well (PHG §§ 464–83; PR § 144, 166). Recall that at the beginning of the play, Antigone's two brothers, Eteocles and Polynices are dead. They were supposed to be sharing power in the city of Thebes, but Polynices had backed out of the agreement, left town, and returned with an armed group of followers to fight his brother; at the end of conflict, though, both Eteocles and Polynices lie dead on the battlefield. Their uncle, Creon, takes power of Thebes and has Eteocles buried as a heroic defender of the city, but leaves Polynices' corpse on the battlefield as an appropriate end for a traitor. Antigone feels obligated to bury her brother Polynices, but Creon forbids it; when Antigone buries the body anyway, Creon orders her to be entombed alive. Haemon, Creon's son and Antigone's fiancé, tries to persuade Creon to have Antigone released, but fails in the effort. After seeking counsel from the prophet Tiresias and the chorus, Creon changes his mind, but it is too late; Antigone and Haemon have both committed suicide.

In Hegel's view, *Antigone* reveals a fundamental rupture in Greek society between what we might call the 'law of the family' and the 'law of the state.' The conflict originates because Antigone is pulled in two directions, and after she makes her choice, the tension is between her and Creon. They both feel compelled to act as they do, and both are dogmatic about the truth of the norms they draw on to justify their actions; but the interesting thing, from Hegel's point of view, is that they are both right, because Greek society contained two equally valid, yet incompatible normative visions: one expressed a more traditional conception of normativity based on the family, and the other expressed the normativity of law and the state. The conflict initially appears to be between Creon's 'universal' claims of law and Antigone's 'particular' claims about her brother, but the language of their arguments contains a reversal: Antigone speaks of the 'divine law' and the universal moral claim that 'the dead should be buried,' while Creon appeals to family loyalty in his dispute with Haemon. Hegel was also particularly interested in the brother-sister relationship as the paradigmatic relation of pure recognition, because it was a clear example of 'identity-in-difference': there is a kind of identity between Antigone and Polynices because they are siblings, yet they are obviously different in many ways as well. Antigone must bury her brother, on this reading, as an act of pure recognition; failure to do this would undermine her status as a person, and a fully autonomous moral agent. In any case, Sophocles' play effectively expresses the historically situated whole, which, it turns out, contains an irreconcilable contradiction. To the extent that his audience was pushed to reflect on the normative status of Antigone's and Creon's competing claims, and to consider the possibility that Greece lacked a coherent set of values that could generate a resolution, *Antigone* was a fitting example of art as 'absolute spirit.'

According to Hegel, the ancient world lacked any strong sense of subjectivity and inwardness, which is just to say that they did not have the conceptual resources available to them to think of selfhood in these terms. We moderns take this conception of subjectivity for granted, but in fact, it emerged gradually through history from the legal structure of ancient Roman society, the pagan fabrication of romantic love in the middle ages, Christianity and the Reformation, and the philosophical currents of early modernity. Classical art, Hegel says, was unable to express the focus on inwardness that characterizes the modern conception of subjectivity, which anyway would have been incomprehensible to the ancient Greeks.

Romantic art, though, emerges alongside this modern conception of subjectivity, and tries to represent the inwardness that characterizes it. The early phase of romantic art, in Hegel's view, was almost entirely Christian art that depicted divine love, faith, and spiritual inwardness; this was usually portrayed as a kind of reconciliation between one's inner life, the domain of faith and spirituality, and the real world, the domain of suffering and the flesh. Hegel thinks that, in terms of historical development, Christianity was responsible for developing the conceptual resources that could support this notion of an 'inner' life, and religious art was able to represent this, at least initially.

As the modern conception of subjectivity developed, though, its artistic representation took on an increasingly secular form, since there was no principled reason why one's inner life needed to be connected to religion in any way. According to Hegel, the first phase of secular art that depicted inwardness represented the chivalric virtues of love, honor, and fidelity. Around the twelfth century, European poets and writers started to explore the inner psychology behind human relationships, and emphasized the individual freedom of choice that lies behind a person's commitments to others. So, for example, in Marie de France's *Lanval* or Andreas Capellanus' *The Art of Courtly Love*, the knights that follow the chivalric code are independent agents, free from all external authority, who choose to devote themselves to the person with whom they fall in love. Their experience of love is a kind of inner suffering, longing, and obsession, and it is significant that their relationships were extra-marital: their experience represents an entirely new conception of love as something that is romantic, passionate and freely chosen, which stands in contrast to the established Christian understanding of love and marriage at the time. The art of this period represented the newly emerging conception of individuality, and found full expression in works such as Giovanni Boccaccio's *Decameron* (HAI 564–5, 569; HAII 1106, 1167–78).

The final and fully secularized stage of romantic art, Hegel says, pushed subjectivity to its limit and represented the modern conception of individual freedom. The literary characters of this period are not bound by moral or political ideals, and are interesting mainly because of their complex inner lives, which are full of imagination and passion; they are also interesting because they are reacting to a modern world that is increasingly complex and fragmented. The paradigmatic examples of such characters, Hegel suggests, appear in William Shakespeare's plays. But it is questionable whether this last stage of romantic art is still trying to express humanity's deepest values and interests; these artistic works are certainly expressing a conception of freedom, but they ultimately exhaust their conceptual resources in this attempt, and can then only express idiosyncrasy and the contingencies of ordinary life, in the form of humor, irony, wit, and so on.

At this point, Hegel says, it becomes increasingly clear that only philosophy can take our understanding further, and this is why, in the Introduction to the *Lectures on Aesthetics*, he claims that art has become 'a thing of the past' for us, and that it can no longer serve the same function it once did relative to our highest needs (HA 11). Of course, although this is typically read as a highly provocative claim about the 'death of art,' it is actually just the mild claim that art in the modern world fails to express our highest values in the best way. He still thinks that art is a form of 'absolute spirit' with a sensuous mode of expression that is distinct from religion and philosophy, and he still thinks that art is an important part of modern culture. And it may be that modern art has an important function in showing us the many levels of fragmentation and dispersion that characterize the modern heterogeneous and pluralistic state; even if modern artists are alienated and unable to do more than represent their own idiosyncrasies, their work may still help us understand some of the key features of our world. But it is not just our developing understanding of freedom, or the fragmentation of the modern state, that keeps art from expressing our fundamental values in the best way; Christianity is also partially responsible for the 'death of art,' because it has consistently devalued the body, the sensuous, and all that is this-worldly (as opposed to other-worldly). According to the Christian worldview, what matters most about human existence cannot be represented in sensuous form, so if the modern world is generally Christian, then we should expect it to be generally unresponsive to art as well.

But if we recall Hegel's view of the 'end' of history, we can infer that, just as he does not think that empirical history comes to an end, he cannot think that artists will stop producing art, or that art will disappear from the sphere of culture. Moreover, we might consider as well that, for Hegel, our talk of the 'end' of history, or the 'end' of art, cannot entail a prediction about the future; philosophy can only look backwards and offer a reconstructive interpretation of how we got here. We may not be able to imagine a next step in the philosophical narrative, but this does not warrant our claiming that there cannot be one. It is at least possible that, at some point in the future, we will look back on modern art and find something analogous to Sophocles' *Antigone*, that is, a work of art that reveals a fundamental and irresolvable rupture in our world. And if it turns out that we failed to notice this rupture precisely because our religious and philosophical thinking blinded us to it, then art will have once again regained its title as the highest form of 'absolute spirit.'

iii. RELIGION IS FOR EVERYONE

In his early writings, Hegel was a harsh critic of Christianity, arguing that its authoritarianism pulled people away from embracing reason and becoming free. He also suggested that Christianity would further depoliticize an already alienated people as a result of its focus on the afterlife and other superstitions, and its otherworldly orientation in general. One of Hegel's early writings, *The Spirit of Christianity*, seems to change course and explore a positive view of Christianity, but rather than showing a shift in his thinking, it is more likely that this is just an early experiment of his speculative hermeneutics; and when he takes up the internal point of view in this context, he ends up anticipating an argument that will appear in the *Phenomenology* (the 'unhappy consciousness' argument), which shows that belief in the Christian God initiates a process of infantilization, the end result of which is the negation of individuality.

When Hegel was lecturing on religion in Berlin in the 1820s, though, he emphasized the ways that religion helps people to reconcile the contradictions in their lives, feel connected to their communities, overcome individualism and egoism, and embrace a frame of reference that is much broader than ordinary, mundane life. Hegel also returns to the notion that we must try to take up an internal perspective when considering religions, so that we can appreciate the 'rational in the real.' And his *Lectures on the Philosophy of Religion* are a very detailed and comprehensive study of the world's religions, including his interpretation of their historical appearance, and the conceptual scheme he uses to categorize their fundamental views of the world.

Hegel's interpretation of the historical and conceptual development of religion starts by considering those religions that seem to conjoin the spiritual and the natural, which he sometimes calls 'nature religions' or 'religions of immediacy'; and the representative examples of this, he suggests, are Taoism, Buddhism, Hinduism, and a number of African religions, which all share the goal of existing in an immediate relationship with this spiritualized nature. Hegel also describes the 'subjective' religions that contemplate our separation from nature, which include the religions of Persia, Egypt, and Greece, as well as Judaism. The categories Hegel employs here are broad, but he occasionally acknowledges certain distinctive features; for example, Greek religion embraces the 'aesthetic,' and Judaism relates to a 'sublime' God that has no physical form. Roman religion, Hegel says, embraced the interests of humanity over the interests of any external, abstract, or otherworldly God, which in their case led to a 'religion of expediency' and the domination of nature. And finally, Hegel considers Christianity to be the 'consummate religion,' because it is the first and only religion where human consciousness is not opposed to God.

However arbitrary, incomplete, or inaccurate his categories may seem in this case, Hegel's main argument about world religions is essentially about the basic distinction between 'subject' and 'object.' If we imagine that a religious community is the 'subject' and its conception of the 'divine' occupies the position of 'object,' we can make sense of his taxonomy. The 'nature religions' take the 'divine' to be nature, and their project is to seek a relationship of immediacy with it; in other words, they want to dissolve the 'subject' into the 'object.' Roman religion, on the other hand, recognizes only human interests, and so is effectively trying to dissolve the 'object' into the 'subject.' 'Nature religions' and Roman religion are one-sided extremes on this interpretation, so other religions may be characterized as sliding towards one of these extremes of the other. Casting Hegel's analysis of religion in these terms makes it clear why he feels that Christianity is the 'consummate' religion: it is the only religion that seems to dissolve the distinction between 'subject' and 'object.' Indeed, this explains why Hegel is interested in the Christian ideas of the incarnation (Jesus as the incarnate form of God) and the trinity (father-son-holy spirit): he thinks they are cases of subject-object unity.

Despite his endorsement of Christianity as the 'consummate religion,' though, Hegel still rejects superstition, empty ritual, and literalism; and the Christianity he is talking about does not have a transcendent God. In fact, by the time Hegel is through with his conceptual and historical reconstruction of the history of the world's religions, his conception of Christianity has been so radically altered that his *Lectures* invite the charge that he must be an atheist or pantheist. The God that Hegel considers is fully immanent in the world and in human activities; his argument is that we can know the 'mind of God', because if God is the whole of nature and reality, and we are the part of the whole that brings nature to its own self-awareness, then we are the 'mind of God.' If religious thinking posits a transcendent God, Hegel thinks, then it will never be able to take up the 'internal' view of the world, and its 'external' understanding of the world will never get beyond symbolic over-simplification; this argument supports his position in the *Encyclopedia* that religion is subordinate to philosophy because it cannot progress beyond metaphors and 'picture-thinking.'

Hegel's interpretation of Christianity is so unorthodox, with all of his qualifications and reinterpretation, it seems that he has essentially converted it into philosophy; but of course, if it becomes philosophy, then it loses the emotional content that stimulates the passions. Although the conceptual clarity of philosophy is a higher form of understanding, Hegel shows in the *Lectures* that he is still interested in the idea that religion, Christianity in particular, had something to offer that philosophy could not: the emotionally-infused experience of participating in a zealous form of social self-understanding that reaches for the whole. This was a concern for Hegel as early as the 'Tübingen essay' and *The Earliest System-Programme*, and one that obviously stuck with him throughout his career; 'religion,' he says, 'is for everyone. It is not philosophy, which is not for everyone' (LPRI 180). But the lingering question here, which Hegel never adequately addresses, is whether his version of religion can really be 'for everyone' or not; if his philosophical version of religion is 'not for everyone,' then his 'system' may require alterations that he, at least, was unable to contemplate.

iv. THE PRACTICE OF PHILOSOPHY

Hegel thinks that philosophy is the highest form of 'absolute spirit' because, unlike art and religion, it has the conceptual resources most appropriate to its object, which is the whole structured and dynamic unity of the world. Art and religion also attempt to grasp the whole, but only philosophy, says Hegel, can unify the content of art and religion, and even render this unity into a simple 'spiritual' vision; and when one finds this unity, he adds, there is a sense in which the 'absolute' practice of philosophy is already underway (ENC III §§ 572). It is important to emphasize that, in Hegel's view, 'absolute spirit' is a practice, not a possession, and a collective social project, not a solitary pursuit; it is also worth pointing out that 'absolute' does not mean 'final' or 'complete,' but rather implies that we are right up against the limit of what we can do. Philosophy that is genuinely systematic and scientific is always pushing this limit, seeking to reconstruct the most basic structure and organizing principles of reality, and hoping for the eventual convergence of the structure of thought and the structure of the world. We should also remember that Hegel's understanding of philosophy is broad and inclusive, and that he distinguishes between 'ordinary' scientists, who labor under the constraints of 'the understanding,' and all the other adventurous philosophically-minded folks, who should join the 'absolute' practice of pushing the limits of what we can know (ENCIII § 573).

Of course, Hegel also thought that philosophy had its own identity, and that this identity was worth preserving as a distinctive form of 'absolute spirit.' In this regard, he felt that the study of the history of philosophy was itself a way of doing philosophy and his *Lectures on the History of Philosophy* provide a fascinating review of his own philosophical engagement with the tradition that preceded him. In the same manner that he approached art and religion, Hegel tries to find an organic unity that emerges from a particular historical period, drawing together culture, politics, and philosophy; and also as with art and religion, he tries to reconstruct a necessary progression from one philosophical worldview to the next. Hegel does suggest, though, at the end of his *Lectures*, that his philosophy is the final and true system of philosophy, which implies that he had been using the history of philosophy all along, as a way to justify the truth of his own view. It is easy to read this the wrong way, however, as though it was all a grand exercise in megalomania, but it is important to understand Hegel's intention here.

If philosophy as 'absolute spirit' is the highest form of humanity's reflection on its most important needs, interests, and values, then surely it takes under its purview the developmental history of its own principles. Whatever these most basic concerns are, they did not emerge spontaneously; they each have a history, and part of understanding them completely entails that we also learn about their origin and development. Hegel's *Lectures*, then, are indeed the 'justification' of his own philosophical system, but only in the sense of a self-critical and reflective process of coming to understand the historical development that led up to his ideas. Indeed, every philosopher should delve into the history of his or her ideas, and of course each will think that his or her ideas fare well in the comparison. All philosophers think that the history of philosophy culminates in their view; but only some philosophers, those with humility and sense of history, take the time to attempt a demonstration of this.

A final question that is naturally generated in light of Hegel's conception of 'absolute spirit' is whether philosophy pulls us away from the world, into some kind of overly-intellectual, detached state of quietist contemplation. One reason to worry about this is Hegel's talk of a 'purely conceptual' grasp of the whole, which leaves one wondering how this grasp would have any connection to practical and worldly affairs; another reason to worry is that his view repeatedly implies that our personal and idiosyncratic interests and projects are of infinitesimal significance compared to the grand import of the whole. Hegel tells us that 'absolute spirit' represents a kind of reflection that is more general than any concern of the state or politics, which would anyway fall under the rubric of 'objective spirit,' and when we add to this his comments in the Preface to the *Philosophy of Right*, that philosophy only seeks to retrospectively comprehend, we can easily conclude that philosophy requires a disengagement from the world.

But for Hegel, 'absolute spirituality' is the unity of 'subjective' and 'objective spirit,' and freedom as self-realization ultimately implies something like the convergence of theory and practice through reflective identification and participation in 'ethical life' (ENCIII §§ 481, 513; PR § 22). It is true that this kind of reflection is more general then the reflection of 'objective spirit,' but this just means that it does not rely on anything external, arbitrary, or 'positive'; 'absolute' reflection aspires to be self-grounding and self-justifying (PR § 23). Art, religion, and philosophy are those practices of self-reflection that do the best job of helping us evaluate our most fundamental values and interests, and are especially effective at turning our attention to the whole, and to the way that all of our different projects are related to each other and mediated by the structured dynamic unity of the world. Our motivations for thinking philosophically will be worldly; and our philosophical thinking can change the world. Hegel writes:

> The need to understand logic in a deeper sense than that of the science of merely formal thinking is sparked by the interests of religion, of the State, of law, and of ethical life. In earlier times people saw no harm in thinking and happily used their own heads. They thought about God, nature, and the State, and were convinced that only by thinking would they become cognizant of

what the truth is, not through the senses or through some chance notion or opinion. But, because they pushed on with thinking in this way, it turned out that the highest relationships in life were compromised by it. Thinking deprived what was positive of its power. Political constitutions fell victim to thought; religion was attacked by thought; firm religious notions that counted as totally genuine revelations were undermined, and in many minds the old faith was overthrown. For example, the Greek philosophers set themselves against the old religion and destroyed its representations. Consequently, philosophers were banished and killed for seeking to overthrow religion and the State . . . In this way thinking asserted its validity in the actual world and exerted the most tremendous influence. (ENCI § 19)

FURTHER READING

There are many comprehensive Hegel bibliographies in print and online, and what follows here is, in comparison, very selective. My suggestions for further reading are informed by my years of experience teaching Hegel to college students, and reflect my own pedagogical approach to Hegelian philosophy. I would think that the best context for new readers of Hegel to continue working through his philosophy would be a university course on nineteenth-century Philosophy, where students and professor can discuss the text on an ongoing basis, over the course of a few months, and can place his ideas in their historical context; but of course, a serious reading group outside of a university setting can work just as well. In either case, it might be best to start with an edited selection of Hegel's texts.

EDITED SELECTIONS

M. J. Inwood's edited collection, *Hegel: Selections* (New York: Macmillan Publishing Co., 1989), is fine, but I prefer, and use in the courses I teach, Stephen Houlgate's *The Hegel Reader* (Malden, MA: Blackwell Publishing, 1998), in part because it has selections from Hegel's early writings. There are usually extensive Hegel selections in any nineteenth-century Philosophy readers as well; for example: Baird and Kaufmann's *Philosophical Classics, Vol. IV: Nineteenth-Century Philosophy, 3rd Edition* (Upper Saddle River, NJ: Prentice Hall, 1999), though a more recent option that may become equally popular is Kolak and Thompson's *The Longman Standard History of Nineteenth-Century Philosophy* (Upper Saddle River, NJ: Longman, 2007).

GENERAL INTERPRETATIONS

There are a number of excellent comprehensive interpretations of Hegel's philosophy, and these are longer books that are appropriate for scholars, intellectually-minded general readers, and serious or advanced students. Of the 'classics' in this category, the most helpful and interesting are Charles Taylor's *Hegel* (Cambridge: Cambridge University Press, 1975), John Findlay's *Hegel: A Re-examination* (Oxford: Oxford University Press, 1976), and Walter Kaufmann's *Hegel: A Reinterpretation* (Notre Dame, IN: University of Notre Dame Press, 1988). Two more recent excellent books are Frederick Beiser's *Hegel* (London: Routledge, 2005) and Stephen Houlgate's *An Introduction to Hegel: Freedom, Truth, and History, 2nd Edition* (Malden, MA: Blackwell Publishing, 2005). These last two books attempt to be both an introduction appropriate for first-timers and a challenging and interesting read for Hegel experts, and while I do think their authors have done as well as can be imagined, they have steered the content of their books (perhaps more than they realize) towards issues that Hegel experts recognize immediately, but that leave many undergraduates bewildered.

SHORT INTRODUCTIONS

There are some more accessible and shorter introductions to Hegel, which have similar aims as this book, but that emphasize different themes; for example, Peter Singer's *Hegel: A Very Short Introduction* (Oxford: Oxford University Press, 2001), Raymond Plant's *Hegel* (London: Routledge, 1999), and Alison Leigh Brown's *On Hegel* (Wadsworth Philosophers Series, 2000), are each helpful in different ways. Since these books are too short to be comprehensive treatments of Hegel's philosophy, they must use some thematic approach or other to limit the material they consider. So, for example, the thematic emphasis of Plant's book connects Hegel with major questions in the philosophy of religion. A slightly longer introductory book is Michael Allen Fox's *The Accessible Hegel* (Atlantic Highlands, NJ: Humanities Press, 2005), which focuses on Hegel's methodology to characterize and unify his various works and interests; it seems to me, however, that this is already less than optimally accessible to new students of philosophy: students just coming to philosophy will find it difficult to appreciate why Hegel's method of doing philosophy is so interesting, because they will have no developed intuitions about how philosophy should be done, nor any familiarity with how philosophy has been done up until Hegel (say, by Socrates, or Plato, or Descartes, and so on).

INTELLECTUAL HISTORY

Books that cover the broad historical, intellectual, and in some cases biographical, context of Hegel's philosophy are especially helpful, because they connect his thinking to the major issues of his day and make it possible to understand what his distinctive contributions are. The best, in my view, are: Frederick Beiser's *The Fate of Reason: German Philosophy from Kant to Fichte* (Cambridge, MA: Harvard University Press, 1987) and *German Idealism: The Struggle Against Subjectivism, 1781–1801* (Cambridge, MA: Harvard University Press, 1996); Terry Pinkard's *German Philosophy 1760–1860: The Legacy of Idealism* (Cambridge: Cambridge University Press, 2002); Tom Rockmore's *Before & After Hegel: A Historical Introduction to Hegel's Thought* (Berkeley, CA: University of California Press, 1993); William Schroeder's *Continental Philosophy: A Critical Approach* (Malden, MA: Blackwell Publishing, 2005); Richard Schacht's *Hegel and After: Studies in Continental Philosophy between Kant and Sartre* (Pittsburgh, PA: University of Pittsburgh, 1975); and Robert Solomon's *Continental Philosophy since 1750* (Oxford: Oxford University Press, 1988). And Terry Pinkard's book, *Hegel: A Biography* (Cambridge: Cambridge University Press, 2000), is well worth reading as well. Anyone who is looking for more about Hegel's early writings might consider Laurence Dickey's *Hegel: Religion, Economics, and the Politics of Spirit 1770–1806* (Cambridge: Cambridge University Press, 1987) and Georg Lukács' *The Young Hegel: Studies in the Relations between Dialectics and Economics*, translated by Rodney Livingstone (Cambridge: MIT Press, 1976).

EDITED COLLECTIONS

For anyone moving into the secondary literature on Hegel, it would be wise first to tackle a broad sampling from influential interpreters and commentators, and there are a number of good edited collections of journal articles including: Frederick Beiser's *The Cambridge Companion to Hegel* (Cambridge: Cambridge University Press, 1993), Ardis Collins' *Hegel on the Modern World* (Albany, NY: State University of New York Press, 1995), Jon Stewart's *The Hegel Myths and Legends* (Evanston, IL: Northwestern University Press, 1996); Alasdair MacIntyre's *Hegel: A Collection of Critical Essays* (Garden City, NY: Doubleday & Co., Inc., 1972), L. S. Stepelevich's *Selected Essays on G.W.F. Hegel* (Atlantic Highlands, NJ: Humanities Press, 1993), and Shaun Gallagher's *Hegel, History, and Interpretation* (Albany, NY: State University of New York Press, 1997). Students trying to figure out how Hegel's philosophy connects with the typical concerns of analytic philosophy should read Tom Rockmore's *Hegel, Idealism, and Analytic Philosophy* (New Haven, CT: Yale University Press, 2005).

THE *PHENOMENOLOGY OF SPIRIT*

Hegel's *Phenomenology of Spirit* has been a very influential book, and there are a number of excellent commentaries on it; and I do suggest that one read the *Phenomenology* with others in a class or reading group, and that one make use of one or two of these commentaries. The most accessible of these is Robert Solomon's *In the Spirit of Hegel* (Oxford: Oxford University Press, 1983); other excellent commentaries are Terry Pinkard's *Hegel's Phenomenology: the Sociality of Reason* (Cambridge: Cambridge University Press, 1994), Michael Forster's *Hegel's Idea of a Phenomenology of Spirit* (Chicago, IL: University of Chicago Press, 1998), and Robert Pippin's *Hegel's Idealism: the Satisfactions of Self-Consciousness* (Cambridge: Cambridge University Press, 1998). Walter Kaufmann's commentary on the Preface to Hegel's *Phenomenology*, in his book *Hegel: Texts and Commentary* (Notre Dame, IN: University of Notre Dame Press, 1989) is also very helpful. And given his influence on twentieth-century interpretation of Hegel, Alexandre Koéve's book, *Introduction to the Reading of Hegel: Lectures of the Phenomenology of Spirit*, translated by James Nichols (Ithaca, NY: Cornell University Press, 1969), is essential. In fact, related to Koéve's reading of Hegel, there are a number of interesting books that work with Hegel's account of 'pure' or 'mutual' recognition, and though most of these stretch well beyond the confines of the *Phenomenology*, they all use that text as a touchstone. Some of these are: Robert Williams, *Hegel's Ethics of Recognition* (Berkeley, CA: University of California Press, 1997) and *Recognition: Fichte and Hegel on the Other* (New York: State University of New York Press, 1992); John O'Neill, *Hegel's Dialectic of Desire and Recognition* (Albany, NY: State University of New York Press, 1996); and Paul Redding's *Hegel's Hermeneutics* (Ithaca, NY: Cornell University Press, 1996).

SOCIAL AND POLITICAL PHILOSOPHY

The last thirty years or so has seen a surge of Hegel scholarship in English, and most of the new writing has concerned his social and political philosophy. There are many excellent books in this area, and the best place to begin is Charles Taylor's *Hegel and the Modern State* (Cambridge: Cambridge University Press, 1979), in part because this book shares arguments with Taylor's *Hegel*, which connects political claims to Hegel's more general view. Some excellent recent books are: Allen Wood's *Hegel's Ethical Thought* (Cambridge: Cambridge University Press, 1990), Michael Hardimon's *Hegel's Social Philosophy: the Project of Reconciliation* (Cambridge: Cambridge University Press, 1994), Paul Franco's *Hegel's Philosophy of Freedom* (New Haven, CT: Yale University Press, 1999),

Frederick Neuhouser's *Foundations of Hegel's Social Theory: Actualizing Freedom* (Cambridge, MA: Harvard University Press, 2000), and Stephen B. Smith's *Hegel's Critique of Liberalism: Rights in Context* (Chicago, IL: University of Chicago Press, 1989). Also good are: Alan Patten's *Hegel's Idea of Freedom* (Oxford: Oxford University Press, 1999) and Terry Pinkard's *Democratic Liberalism and Social Union* (Philadelphia, PA: Temple University Press, 1987). Joseph McCarney's *Hegel on History* (London: Routledge, 2002) is very good. Two notable books on Hegel and feminism are: Jeffery Gauthier's *Hegel and Feminist Social Theory: Justice, Recognition, and the Feminine* (Albany, NY: State University of New York Press, 1997) and Patricia Mills, ed., *Feminist Interpretations of G.W.F. Hegel* (Pennsylvania, PA: Pennsylvania State University Press, 1996).

There are also a number of helpful journal articles that address Hegel's social and political philosophy, some of which are in collections: L. S. Stepelevich, ed. *Selected Essays on G.W.F. Hegel* (Atlantic Highlands, NJ: Humanities Press, 1993), Pippin and Hoeffe, eds, *Hegel on Ethics and Politics* (Cambridge: Cambridge University Press, 2004), and Cornell, Rosenfeld, and Carlson, eds, *Hegel and Legal Theory* (London: Routledge, 1991). One article that is relevant to the augments of this book is Norbert Waszek's 'Eduard Gans on Poverty: Between Hegel and Saint-Simon,' in *The Owl of Minerva* (Vol. 18, no. 2). I also have a number of articles on Hegel available in various places: 'Hegel's Idea of Freedom,' available on *Blackwell Philosophy Compass* (www.blackwell-compass.com), which has a growing database of peer-reviewed essays on all philosophical topics, 'Solidarity and Fear: Hegel and Sartre on the Mediations of Reciprocity,' *Philosophy Today* (Vol. 45:1 – Spring 2001), and 'Satisfaction or Supersession? Expression, Rationality, and Irony in Hegel and Rorty,' *Clio* (Vol. 36: 1 – Fall 2006).

OTHER TOPICS

There are a number of good books on other areas of Hegel's philosophy, but as I mentioned, the literature on his social and political philosophy is much more developed. Worth mentioning, however, are: Terry Pinkard's *Hegel's Dialectic: the Explanation of Possibility* (Philadelphia, PA: Temple University Press, 1988), Alison Stone's *Petrified Intelligence: Nature in Hegel's Philosophy* (Albany, NY: State University of New York Press, 2005), and Stephen Houlgate, ed. *Hegel and the Philosophy of Nature* (Albany, NY: State University of New York Press, 1998).

INDEX